REVISE EDEXCEL GCSE (9–1)
German

REVISION GUIDE

Series Consultant: Harry Smith

Author: Harriette Lanzer

A note from the publisher

In order to ensure that this resource offers high-quality support for the associated Pearson qualification, it has been through a review process by the awarding body. This process confirms that this resource fully covers the teaching and learning content of the specification or part of a specification at which it is aimed. It also confirms that it demonstrates an appropriate balance between the development of subject skills, knowledge and understanding, in addition to preparation for assessment.

Endorsement does not cover any guidance on assessment activities or processes (e.g. practice questions or advice on how to answer assessment questions), included in the resource nor does it prescribe any particular approach to the teaching or delivery of a related course.

While the publishers have made every attempt to ensure that advice on the qualification and its assessment is accurate, the official specification and associated assessment guidance materials are the only authoritative source of information and should always be referred to for definitive guidance.

Pearson examiners have not contributed to any sections in this resource relevant to examination papers for which they have responsibility.

Examiners will not use endorsed resources as a source of material for any assessment set by Pearson.

Endorsement of a resource does not mean that the resource is required to achieve this Pearson qualification, nor does it mean that it is the only suitable material available to support the qualification, and any resource lists produced by the awarding body shall include this and other appropriate resources.

Difficulty scale

The scales next to each exam-style question tells you how difficult it is.

Some questions cover a range of difficulties The more of the scale that is shaded, the harder the question is.

 Some questions are Foundation level.

 Some questions are Higher level.

 Some questions are applicable to both levels.

For the full range of Pearson revision titles across KS2, KS3, GCSE, Functional Skills, AS/A Level and BTEC visit:
www.pearsonschools.co.uk/revise

LONDON BOROUGH OF BARNET

D0358063

Contents

1-to-1 page match with the German Revision Workbook ISBN 9781292131351

AUDIO

Audio files for the listening exercises in this book can be accessed by using the QR codes or hotlinks, or going to www.pearsonschools.co.uk/mflrevisionaudio throughout the book.

Listen to the recording

A small bit of small print

Edexcel publishes Sample Assessment Material and the Specification on its website. This is the official content and this book should be used in conjunction with it. The questions in Now try this have been written to help you practise every topic in the book. Remember: the real exam questions may not look like this.

Physical descriptions

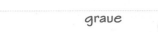

You will need to describe people in the photo task of the Speaking exam, so make sure you have lots of this handy vocabulary at your fingertips!

Wie sieht er / sie aus?

Er / Sie hat … Haare.	He / She has … hair.
blonde	graue
braune	schwarze
dunkle / helle	dark / light
glatte / lockige	straight / curly
kurze / lange	short / long

Sie hat (blaue) Augen. — She has (blue) eyes.

Er trägt eine Brille. — He is wearing glasses.

Sie trägt große Ohrringe. — She is wearing / wears big earrings.

Er hat einen Bart / Schnurrbart. — He's got a beard / moustache.

Sie hat ein rundes / hübsches Gesicht. — She has a round / pretty face.

Er hat eine Glatze. — He is bald.

Comparing things

Grammar page 90

- For regular comparatives add -er to the adjective:

attraktiv ➡	attraktiver
dick(er)	fat(ter)
hässlich(er)	ugly (uglier)
hübsch(er)	pretty (prettier)
schlank(er)	slim(mer)
schön(er)	(more) beautiful

- The following are irregular:

alt ➡	älter	(old / older)
groß ➡	größer	(big / bigger)
gut ➡	besser	(good / better)
hoch ➡	höher	(high / higher)
jung ➡	jünger	(young / younger)

- Use als to compare:

Ich bin älter als du. I am older than you.

Worked example

READING

Person gesucht
Lies den Bericht.

Person gesucht

Die Polizei sucht dringend einen Kerl. Können Sie uns helfen, ihn zu finden? Der Jugendliche ist im Alter von 17–18 Jahren mit langen, dunkelbraunen und ziemlich lockigen Haaren. Er trägt einen kleinen Ohrring im linken Ohr und hat eine bunte Tätowierung am rechten Arm. Er trägt eine blaue Jeans und ein schwarzes T-Shirt und vielleicht trägt er auch eine grüne Mütze. Er ist sehr gefährlich – bitte rufen Sie sofort bei der Polizei an, falls Sie ihn sehen.

Fülle die Lücke in jedem Satz mit einem Wort oder Wörtern aus dem Kasten. Es gibt mehr Wörter als Lücken.

Beispiel: Die Polizei sucht *einen Mann* .

sprechen	Hobbys	ein Piercing	lang	Kleidung	sechzehn
~~einen Mann~~	zwanzig	glatt	ein Mädchen	weglaufen	eine Glatze

Gender gives you a clue here – the police are looking for **einen Kerl** (masculine accusative) and **der Jugendliche** (masculine nominative) – so the answer cannot be **ein Mädchen** as that is neuter. It has to be **einen Mann** – a male person.

Exam alert

Remember – just because a word is mentioned in the text does not mean that it is the right answer! Read the passage carefully to ensure you understand correctly.

Now try this

READING

Now complete the reading activity.

(a) Der Mann ist jünger als …………… Jahre alt. **(1 mark)**

(b) Seine Haare sind …………… **(1 mark)**

(c) Er hat …………… **(1 mark)**

(d) Die Polizei beschreibt seine …………… **(1 mark)**

(e) Man soll mit dem Mann nicht …………… **(1 mark)**

Character descriptions

To talk about character, you need to be confident with the verb **sein** and know plenty of adjectives to go with it!

Charakterbeschreibung

Ich bin ...	I am ...
altmodisch	old-fashioned
blöd	silly
böse	angry / cross
egoistisch	selfish
ehrlich	honest
ernst	serious
frech	cheeky
freundlich	friendly
gemein	mean / nasty
großartig	awesome
komisch	funny
lieb	likeable / nice
nervig	annoying
nett	nice
optimistisch	optimistic
schüchtern	shy
sympathisch	nice
vernünftig	reasonable
Ich bin humorlos.	I have no sense of humour.

The verb sein (to be)

ich	bin	I am
du	bist	you are
er / sie / es	ist	he / she / it is
wir	sind	we are
ihr	seid	you are
Sie / sie	sind	you / they are

Imperfect tense

ich war (I was)   sie waren (they were)

Eva ist intelligent, aber faul.
Eva is clever but lazy.

You may well need to distinguish between past and present characteristics:

Obwohl er heute frech ist, war er als Kind sehr schüchtern. Although he **is** cheeky today, he **was** very shy as a child.

Worked example

Lauras Freunde
Du hörst einen Bericht im Internet über Lauras Freunde in der Grundschule.

Wie waren sie? Trage entweder **faul**, **freundlich**, **laut** oder **lustig** ein.

Beispiel: Thomas war  lustig.

— Thomas finde ich super, denn bei ihm konnte man immer gut lachen. Er war sehr humorvoll und das habe ich echt gut gefunden.

Listen to the recording

You don't hear the word **lustig**, but understand the whole sentence and you will be able to identify the characteristic!

Aiming higher

Give your work an edge by including one or two of these Higher level adjectives in your writing / speaking.

angeberisch	pretentious
ausgeglichen	well-balanced
deprimiert	depressed
eingebildet	conceited
großzügig	generous
selbstbewusst	self-confident
verrückt	mad / crazy
zuverlässig	reliable

Listen to the recording

Now try this

Now complete the listening activity by writing the correct adjective to complete each sentence.

(a) Laura findet Nils .... **(1 mark)**
(b) Yasmin war früher .... **(1 mark)**
(c) Yasmin ist jetzt sehr .... **(1 mark)**
(d) Claudia war früher nicht .... **(1 mark)**
(e) Laura findet die Zeit mit Claudia.............. **(1 mark)**

Family

Make sure you have a good supply of family-related vocabulary at your disposal!

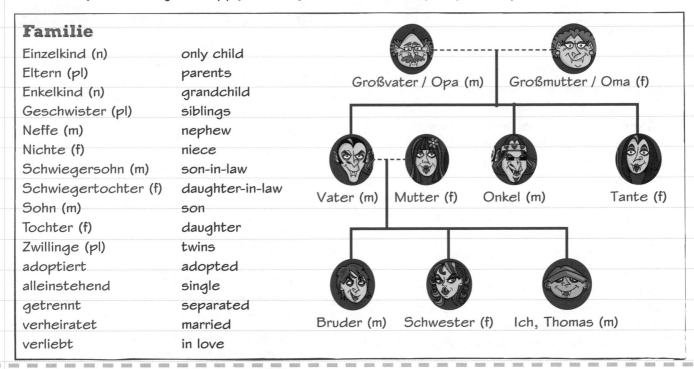

Familie

Einzelkind (n)	only child
Eltern (pl)	parents
Enkelkind (n)	grandchild
Geschwister (pl)	siblings
Neffe (m)	nephew
Nichte (f)	niece
Schwiegersohn (m)	son-in-law
Schwiegertochter (f)	daughter-in-law
Sohn (m)	son
Tochter (f)	daughter
Zwillinge (pl)	twins
adoptiert	adopted
alleinstehend	single
getrennt	separated
verheiratet	married
verliebt	in love

Großvater / Opa (m)   Großmutter / Oma (f)

Vater (m) Mutter (f)   Onkel (m)   Tante (f)

Bruder (m) Schwester (f) Ich, Thomas (m)

Worked example

Deine Familie

Beantworte diese Frage:

- Wie ist deine Familie?

> In meiner Familie gibt es meine Mutter und meinen jüngeren Bruder.

Aiming higher

> Als wir jünger waren, musste meine Mutter ab und zu auf Dienstreise gehen, also hat meine Großmutter auf uns aufgepasst. Das hat Spaß gemacht, weil wir immer viel Zeit beim Keksebacken in der Küche verbracht haben. Nächstes Jahr werden wir nach Amerika fliegen, um unsere Tante dort zu besuchen. Sie ist die Schwester meiner Mutter, und sie ist sehr lustig, also wird es mich freuen, sie zu sehen. Ich persönlich würde gern in Kanada wohnen, aber ich würde meine Familie kaum sehen, und das wäre schlecht.

Improve your speaking by adding adverbs of time, such as **oft**, **ab und zu** and **immer**.

Tenses

In the Speaking exam, include as many tenses as possible when discussing your family:

- ✓ who your family consists of – in the **present**
- ✓ description of an occasion with a family member – in the **past**
- ✓ your family plans – in the **future**
- ✓ something you would like to change about your family – in the **conditional**.

To show excellent knowledge of German, see if you can include the **pluperfect** tense!

Use a genitive to describe who's who in your family: **die Schwester meiner Mutter** – my mother's sister.

Pluperfect suggestion for this student: **Als Kind hatte mein Vater Urlaub in Amerika gemacht, aber er konnte es dort nicht ausstehen!**

Now try this

Now prepare a description of your family, using the example above to help you. Can you talk about them for **one** minute?

Use the advice above to help you include different tenses. Can you fit the pluperfect in too?

Friends

Are friends more important to you than family? What should your best friend be like?

Freunde

Freunde finde ich sehr wichtig.
I find friends very important.
Wir kommen gut miteinander aus.
We get on well with each other.
Mit guten Freunden ist man nie einsam.
You are never lonely with good friends.
Ich kenne meine beste Freundin seit der Grundschule.
I have known my best friend since primary school.
Unsere Freundschaft ist sehr stark.
Our friendship is very strong.
Es ist mir egal, ob meine Freunde reich oder arm sind.
I don't care if my friends are rich or poor.
Die ideale Freundin / Der ideale Freund sollte meiner Meinung nach lieb und sportlich sein.
The ideal friend, in my opinion, should be kind and sporty.

Using sollte (should)

Grammar page 98

sollte + infinitive

ich sollte	wir sollten
du solltest	ihr solltet
er / sie sollte	Sie / sie sollten

Ein guter Freund sollte treu sein.
A good friend should be loyal.
Ein guter Freund sollte …
A good (male) friend should …
Eine gute Freundin sollte …
A good (female) friend should …
… geduldig sein.
… be patient.
… immer Zeit für mich haben.
… always have time for me.
… dieselben Interessen wie ich haben.
… have the same interests as me.
… nie schlechter Laune sein.
… never be in a bad mood.
… immer guter Laune sein.
… always be in a good mood.

Worked example

WRITING

Freunde
Übersetze **ins Deutsche**. **(2 marks)**

My best friend, Max, is quite sporty and happy.

Mein bester Freund, Max, ist ziemlich sportlich und glücklich.

In German you need to identify the gender of a 'friend': **der Freund** – male friend / boyfriend; **die Freundin** – female friend / girlfriend.

Translating into German

If you just can't think of the word for the translation, don't panic, but try one of these strategies:

- Do you know the German for the **opposite** word? If you have forgotten the German for 'happy', use the opposite, traurig (sad), instead, with the negative nie: nie traurig = never sad = happy.
- Can you **change** an adjective into a verbal phrase? For example, if your best friend is sporty and you can't remember the adjective, you could say er mag Sport or er treibt gern Sport.
- Can you perhaps use a word **similar** to English? Sporty could equally be aktiv, a very similar word to one in English, which conveys the same meaning.

Now try this

WRITING

Now translate these sentences **into German**.

(a) My friend Carol is clever and very funny. **(2 marks)**
(b) I often see my friends after school. **(2 marks)**
(c) Last week my boyfriend had a party. **(3 marks)**
(d) My best friend lived in Spain when she was eight years old. **(3 marks)**

You need the German word for 'female friend' here, as it is a 'she'! Remember that **als** (when) in the past tense sends the verb to the end of the clause.

Role models

Do you have a role model? What can you say about him / her? Look at this page for some ideas.

Vorbilder

Mein Vorbild …	My role model …
ist ein Familienmitglied.	is a family member.
kommt aus meinem Freundschaftskreis. comes from my friendship group.	
ist ein/e Sportler/in.	is a sports person.
ist ein Star.	is a celebrity / star.
versucht, die Welt besser zu machen. tries to make the world better.	
hilft anderen Menschen.	helps other people.
Charakter (m)	character
Leben (n)	life
Persönlichkeit (f)	personality, character
abenteuerlich / unternehmungslustig	adventurous
selbstsicher	self-confident
sensibel / empfindlich	sensitive
verwöhnt / verdorben	spoilt
Respekt haben (vor)	to respect

The verb haben (to have)

Present tense

ich	habe	I have
du	hast	you have
er / sie / es	hat	he / she / it has
wir	haben	we have
ihr	habt	you have
Sie / sie	haben	you / they have

Use the verb haben to add variety to your sentences:

Ich habe kein Vorbild, aber ich hätte gern eins.

I don't have a role model but I would like one.

Imperfect tense
ich hatte (I had)
wir hatten (we had)

Perfect tense
ich habe / er hat … gehabt
(I have / he has had …)

Worked example

Role models
Read this article from a German newspaper.

> Vorbilder können Jugendlichen motivieren. Es kann ihnen auch gelingen, die Träume von ihren Fans in Wirklichkeit zu bringen. Sie helfen der jüngeren Generation, das Beste aus ihren Charaktereigenschaften zu machen. Jeder Einzelne findet sein einziges Vorbild je nach Geschmack in einem bestimmten Lebensbereich.
>
> Manche Jugendliche wählen sich ein Vorbild aus der Film- oder Musikwelt aus, um ihre eigene Fähigkeiten zu verbessern. Einige finden ihren Helden im Sportkreis, denn solche Stars helfen ihnen, das persönliche sportliche Ziel zu erreichen. Die letzte Gruppe sucht sich Lehrer, Naturschützer, Wissenschaftler oder Schriftsteller aus, weil diese etwas in der Welt verändert haben.

Answer the question **in English**.
Give one example of a positive effect role models have on people.

(1 mark)

Role models help people achieve their dreams.

Exam alert

Don't be distracted by plurals of familiar words: **der Traum** = dream, **Träume** = dreams!

Break down long words to get to the meaning: **Leben + Bereich = Lebensbereich** (part of life).

Watch out for words like **manche** and **einige** which can both be translated as 'some'.

You need to say that role models 'help people achieve their dreams' – just 'achieve dreams' is not enough.

Now try this

Now answer these questions on the text **in English**.
You do not need to write in full sentences.
(a) Why do role models come from a variety of areas? **(1 mark)**
(b) Give **one** effect of a celebrity role model on somebody. **(1 mark)**
(c) Give **two** examples of role models who have changed something. **(2 marks)**

Relationships

Talking about different people requires not just a matching verb ending, but also a matching possessive pronoun. Make sure you can apply these in your writing and speaking tasks.

Possessive adjectives

Grammar page 88

Possessive pronouns use the same endings as ein and kein.

mein	my	unser	our
dein	your	euer	your (plural familiar)
sein	his	Ihr	your (polite)
ihr	her	ihr	their

Masculine
Ich liebe meinen Hund.   I love my dog.

Feminine
Ihre Katze ist so süß.   Her cat is so sweet.

Neuter
Er mag sein Meerschweinchen sehr.
He likes his guinea pig a lot.

Plural
Wo sind eure Mäuse?   Where are your mice?

Beziehungen

(Mein Bruder) nervt mich / geht mir auf die Nerven.
(My brother) annoys me.

Wir streiten uns ständig. We always argue.

Ich kann (meine Tante) nicht ausstehen.
I can't stand (my aunt).

Ich komme gut / schlecht mit (den Lehrern) aus.
I get on well / badly with (the teachers).

Ich verstehe mich gut mit (der Klasse).
I get on well with (the class).

Ich stehe / bleibe in Kontakt mit (meinen Cousinen).
I am / stay in contact with (my cousins).

Ich lerne gern neue Leute kennen.
I like getting to know new people.

Ich fühle mich (meinem Opa) sehr verbunden.
I feel very close to (my grandad).

(Meine Mutti) ist mir wichtig.
(My mum) is important to me.

Ich kann mich auf (meine Schwester) verlassen.
I can rely on (my sister).

Worked example

Listen to the recording

Wichtige Leute
Du hörst dieses Interview im Radio.

Fülle die Lücke in jedem Satz mit einem Wort oder Wörtern aus dem Kasten. Es gibt mehr Wörter als Lücken.

Beispiel: Hakans ...Oma... verbringt viele Stunden mit ihm.

mag	dreimal	45	Lehrer	Schüler	54	Mutter
Freunde	viermal	~~Oma~~	hasst	Hobbys		

— Meine Mutter arbeitet lange Stunden, also ist meine Oma mir besonders wichtig. Sie hat immer Zeit für mich.

Exam alert

Before you listen, identify the two words from the box that work grammatically in each gap. Then listen to find out which of those two words is correct.

Don't jump to the wrong conclusion: just because Hakan mentions **Mutter** in the interview, it does not mean this must be the answer.

Now try this

Now listen to the rest of the recording and complete the sentences.
(a) Im Moment hat Hakan ein Problem mit einem .... **(1 mark)**
(b) Hakan ist gestern ...... Minuten extra in der Schule geblieben. **(1 mark)**
(c) Hakan hat seine Hausaufgaben ...... nicht gemacht. **(1 mark)**
(d) Hakan hat viele .... **(1 mark)**
(e) Hakan ...... die Schule aufgrund seiner Freunde. **(1 mark)**

Listen to the recording

When I was younger

Use different pronouns with the matching verb ending to add variety to your work.

Die Kindheit

Ich bin in (Wien) geboren.
I was born in (Vienna).
Er hatte oft Ärger in der Schule.
He was often in trouble at school.
Sie war ein stures Kind.
She was a stubborn child.
Wir durften nicht alleine zur Schule gehen.
We weren't allowed to go to school on our own.
Ich musste keine Hausaufgaben machen.
I didn't have to do any homework.
Mit acht Jahren konnte ich (schwimmen).
At eight years old I could (swim).
Er wollte (Feuerwehrmann) werden.
He wanted to be (a fireman).

Pronouns

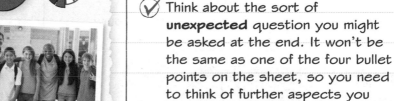

Grammar page 91

Pronouns = he, him, their, her, your, our

nominative	accusative	dative
ich	mich	mir
du	dich	dir
er	ihn	ihm
sie	sie	ihr
es	es	ihm
wir	uns	uns
ihr	euch	euch
Sie / sie	Sie / sie	Ihnen / ihnen

Sie war immer gut gelaunt.
She was always in a good mood.
Hast du mich gesehen?   Did you see me?

Worked example

Daily life

Schau dir das Foto an und sei bereit, über Folgendes zu sprechen:

• Deine Meinung dazu, ob die Kindheit eine gute Zeit ist.

Die sechs Kinder im Foto sehen alle sehr glücklich aus, denn es gibt nichts, worüber sie sich Sorgen machen müssen! Sie stehen noch nicht unter Leistungsdruck in der Schule, denn der Schulalltag in der Grundschule ist entspannt und locker. <u>Je älter man wird, desto stressiger wird das Leben</u> und das finde ich schade. In der Klasse neun muss ich jeden Abend entweder Hausaufgaben machen oder für die Klassenarbeiten lernen, aber diese Kinder im Bild müssen das nicht. Sie spielen wahrscheinlich nach der Schule Fußball oder gehen ins Schwimmbad, stelle ich mir vor.

This student has slipped in the idiom je mehr ... desto ... (the more ... the more ...) to raise the level.
Try to include idioms in your work:
entweder ... oder = either ... or
weder ... noch = neither ... nor

Try to speak for at least 30 seconds on each point.

Picture-based task (Higher)

In your preparation time for the picture task:

☑ Think about the sort of **unexpected** question you might be asked at the end. It won't be the same as one of the four bullet points on the sheet, so you need to think of further aspects you could be asked about.

☑ Make sure you can **describe** the photo to begin with, by recalling plenty of relevant adjectives as well as positional words: in der Mitte des Bildes, vor der Tafel, etc.

☑ Use the preparation time to consider the **four** known points, which you have to speak about (see page 57 in the Now try this for an example of these). Spend a few minutes on each point, noting the tenses you can use and any relevant vocabulary, but remember: you **must not** read out whole prepared sentences.

Now try this

Now prepare answers to these unexpected questions you could be asked about the photo.
• Was für Probleme gibt es oft bei Kindern?
• Was war das beste Ereignis aus deiner Kindheit?
• Wie würdest du deine Grundschule verändern?
• Was werden die Kinder im Foto in Zukunft machen, meinst du?

Peer group

Understanding question words is crucial to exam success – make sure you have the answers!

Die Altersgenossen

Alleinstehende (m/f)	single person
Bande / Gruppe (f)	gang / group
Bekannte (m/f)	acquaintance
Beziehung (f)	relationship
Diskriminierung (f)	discrimination
Feier / Party (f)	party
Freundschaft (f)	friendship
Jugend (f)	youth (i.e. time of life)
Jugendliche (m/f)	teenager / adolescent
Typ / Kerl (m)	guy
aussehen wie	to look like
gehören	to belong
mobben / schikanieren	to bully
minderjährig	underage
multikulturell (multikulti)	multicultural
rassistisch	racist
sexistisch	sexist
treu	loyal / faithful
unter Druck stehen	to be under pressure

Make sure you don't confuse **wer?** (who?) with **wo?** (where?).

Question words

Grammar page 106

Wann?	When?
Warum?	Why?
Was?	What?
Wer?	Who?
Wie?	How?
Wo?	Where?
Was für ...?	What sort of...?
Wen? Wem?	Who(m)?
Wessen?	Whose?
Wie viele?	How many?

Justifying opinions

✓ Always **justify** your opinion by adding a weil or denn clause to give the reason for your opinion.

✓ You can also use an um ... zu ... clause to give a reason: Ich hänge gern mit meinen Freunden herum, um Spaß zu haben.

✓ Or start with a justification: Damit wir sicher sind, fahren wir im Bus zusammen zur Party.

Worked example

Question words are used here – but as statements.

Remember to **justify** your ideas and opinions.

Freundschaftsprobleme
Du hast einen neuen Freundschaftskreis, aber es gibt ein Problem mit ihm.

Schreibe einen Brief an eine Zeitschrift, der das Problem erklärt. Du **musst** diese Punkte einschließen:

• was das Problem ist und wann es begonnen hat

• warum Jugendliche Probleme mit Freunden haben

• die Vorteile einer festen Freundschaftsgruppe

• wie man in Zukunft Probleme mit Freunden lösen könnte.

Rechtfertige deine Ideen und Meinungen.

Schreibe ungefähr 130–150 Wörter **auf Deutsch**.

(28 marks)

Letztes Jahr musste ich an einer anderen Schule anfangen, wo ich glücklicherweise schnell neue Freunde in der Klasse kennengelernt habe. Ein Kerl in der Gruppe ist aber rassistisch, und da meine Familie aus der Türkei kommt, hat er ein Problem mit mir.

Now try this

Now prepare your own answers to the four points in the worked example and complete the writing activity.

Aim to write a total of around 130–150 words. Divide the number of words required by the number of points you need to answer.

This is the first part of a student answer, addressing the first bullet.

A modal verb in the imperfect tense is an effective way of introducing the past tense into your work: **musste** = had to.

The use of the conjunctions **wo** and **da** + verb at the end of the clause helps to raise the level of this answer.

Customs

In German-speaking countries, a host parent and even your exchange partner might well shake your hand when they greet you, so be prepared!

Guten Tag!

Wie geht's dir / Ihnen?	How are you?
Entschuldigung	excuse me / sorry
Wie bitte?	Pardon?
bis später	see you later
bis bald	see you soon
guten Abend	good evening
auf Wiedersehen	goodbye
grüß Gott / servus	hello
guten Tag	hello, good day
guten Appetit	enjoy your meal
hallo	hello
Mahlzeit!	enjoy your meal
gute Reise	have a good trip
danke schön	thank you
bitte sehr / schön	you're welcome
Ich bin satt.	I am full.
Bedien dich.	Help yourself.
Es ärgert mich.	It annoys me.
Moment mal.	Wait a moment.
Was bedeutet das?	What does that mean?
Kann ich etwas ausrichten?	Can I take a a message?
Ich verstehe eigentlich nicht.	I don't actually understand.

Qualifiers

If you don't want to appear over-enthusiastic, add a qualifier to your adjectives:

gar nicht	not at all
nicht	not
ein bisschen	a bit
ganz	quite
ziemlich	quite
meistens	mostly
ein wenig	a bit
kaum	hardly
vielleicht	perhaps

Exam alert

Speak clearly during the role play and remember to use the correct register. Follow your teacher's lead, as well as the instruction card, to find out if it is **du** (an informal role play) or **Sie** (a formal role play). Use that register.

In the role play, remember:

- the teacher will speak first
- you will talk to the teacher using the five prompts provided
- where you see – ? – you must ask a question (do not simply repeat the words in the task)
- where you see – ! – you must respond to something you have not prepared.

Worked example

Instructions to candidate: You have just arrived at your exchange family's home in Austria. Your teacher will play the role of your exchange partner and will speak first.

Task

Du bist gerade bei deiner Gastfamilie in Österreich angekommen. Du und dein(e) Austauschpartner(in) lernen einander kennen.

1 Wie es dir geht (zwei Details)
– Hallo. Wie geht's?
– Sehr gut, danke, aber ich bin ein bisschen müde.

2 Essen (zwei Details)
– Möchtest du etwas essen?
– Ja, einen Apfel und Kekse, bitte.

3 ! – Was hast du im Koffer?
– Ich habe meine Kleider.

There are no wrong answers, as long as you respond fully to the bullet point and your answer makes sense. For example, in response to question 3, you could have anything in your suitcase: clothes, books, presents, shoes … Choose words you are confident with.

Now try this

Now practise the whole role play yourself, including the final two prompts. Listen to the audio file containing the teacher's part and fill in the pauses with your answers:

4 Mittagessen: wann und wo
5 ? Abends bei der Gastfamilie

Listen to the recording

9

Home

Use your knowledge of tenses to write about when something **is** happening, **has** happened or **will** happen!

Three key tenses

To aim for the top grades, you need to recognise and use different tenses:

Present tense

- Make sure you know the present tense regular and irregular endings (page 95).

  Ich esse zu Mittag.   I eat / am eating lunch.

  Wir essen zu Mittag.   We eat / are eating lunch.

  Watch out for the present tense implying future meaning.

  Morgen esse ich Pizza zu Mittag.

  Tomorrow I am going to have pizza for lunch.

Das Zuhause

Badezimmer (n)	bathroom
Dusche (f)	shower
Esszimmer (n)	dining room
Küche (f)	kitchen
Schlafzimmer (n)	bedroom
Wohnzimmer (n)	sitting room
Garage (f)	garage
Garten (m)	garden
Haustier (n)	pet
Doppelhaus (n)	semi-detached house
Reihenhaus (n)	terraced house
Wohnung (f)	flat

Past tenses

- Use the correct form of haben and sein + past participle to form the **perfect** tense.

  Ich habe zu Mittag gegessen.

  I ate lunch.

  Er ist in die Küche gegangen.

  He went into the kitchen.

- Use the **imperfect** tense war (was), hatte (had) and es gab (there was / were) for descriptions in the past.

- Use the correct form of haben and sein in the imperfect tense + past participle to form the **pluperfect** tense.

  Ich hatte zu Mittag gegessen.

  I had eaten lunch.

  Er war in die Küche gegangen.

  He had gone into the kitchen.

Future tense

- Use the correct form of werden (to become) + infinitive verb to form the future tense.

  Ich werde zu Mittag essen.

  I will eat lunch.

  Er wird in die Küche gehen.

  He will go into the kitchen.

Worked example

Translation

Translate this passage **into English**.

> Zu Hause darf man nicht im Wohnzimmer essen, obwohl es dort so bequem ist.

At home you are not allowed to eat in the sitting room, although it is so comfortable there.

Remember that **darf** is part of the verb **dürfen** (to be allowed to).

Why is **ist** at the end of the sentence? It's because of **obwohl** (although) earlier on — read the entire sentence **before** you attempt to translate it.

Now try this

Now complete the translation **into English**.

> Meine Eltern sind altmodisch und wir müssen zu Mittag immer zusammen essen und plaudern, weil Handys und sonstige elektronische Geräte am Tisch verboten sind. Mein Traum ist es, alleine in der Stadtmitte zu wohnen, so dass ich meine eigene Hausordnung machen kann. Als Kind habe ich auf dem Land gewohnt, aber das war schrecklich langweilig, weil es abends nichts zu tun gab. Ich möchte nie wieder in so einem Ort wohnen!

Everyday life

You will need to understand both 12- and 24-hour clock times.

Der Alltag

Wir wohnen in einer Wohnung. We live in a flat.

Ich stehe um sechs Uhr auf. I get up at six o'clock.

Ich fahre mit dem Rad zur Schule.
I go by bike to school.

Nachmittags habe ich (keine) Schule.
I (don't) have school in the afternoon.

Um vier Uhr gehe ich in den Sportverein.
I go to the sports club at four o'clock.

Abends bin ich oft online.
I am often online in the evenings.

Um zwei Uhr ist Ruhezeit im Wohnblock.
At two o'clock it is quiet time in the block of flats.

Man darf sonntags nicht Auto waschen.
You are not allowed to wash the car on a Sunday.

Die Geschäfte sind bis acht Uhr abends offen.
The shops are open until eight o'clock in the evenings.

12-hour clock

zwei Uhr

fünf nach zwei

Viertel nach zwei

halb drei

Be careful! **Halb drei** is half past two (literally, half **to** three).

Viertel vor drei

zehn vor drei

Worked example

 LISTENING TRACK 6

Daily life

You hear a radio report about the daily life of modern teenagers.

Listen to the report and answer the following question **in English**.

(a) What is the effect of modern life on teenagers?
(1 mark)

no longer able to concentrate

– Heute berichten wir über Jugendliche. Haben sie wirklich einen Alltag wie früher nur Manager?

– Na ja. Ständig neue Handys, neue Computer, neue Fächer, Nachrichten im Minutentakt und die ganze Welt im Internet: Kein Wunder, dass sich junge Leute nicht mehr konzentrieren können.

Answering questions in English

✓ Use the rubric to guide you into the passage you are going to hear. How many clues can you already pick up from the introductory sentence here?

✓ Ignore the distractors! You may well be chuffed that you understand all the items mentioned, but that is **not** what the question is asking you about.

Make sure you learn time words such as früher / vorher (earlier), später (later) and momentan (at the moment) to help you answer questions precisely. Here, **nicht mehr** means 'no longer' or 'not any more', and that needs to be in your answer.

Now try this

   LISTENING TRACK 7

Now listen to the rest of the report and answer the following questions **in English**.
(b) What has led to teenagers having to act like top managers, according to the report? **(1 mark)**
(c) Give **two** differences between managers and teenagers, according to the report. **(2 marks)**
(d) According to the report, what do teenagers now have to do? **(1 mark)**

Meals at home

Learn a variety of food and drink words so you can talk about food, whatever the time of day!

Mahlzeit!

Abendessen / Abendbrot (n)		supper
Aufschnitt (m)		cold meat
Bratwurst (f)		sausage
Brötchen (n)		bread roll
Ei (n)		egg
Frühstück (n)		breakfast
Gebäck (n)		biscuits
Hähnchen (n)		chicken
Mittagessen (n)		lunch
Obst (n)		fruit
Suppe (f)		soup
Teigwaren / Nudeln (pl)		pasta / noodles

Dative verb schmecken (to taste)

The dative verb schmecken works in the same way as gefallen (to like): es gefällt mir (I like it).

Es schmeckt mir gut.   It tastes good.

Es hat mir nicht geschmeckt.   It didn't taste good.

bitter	bitter
lecker / köstlich	tasty / delicious
sauer	sour
scharf	highly seasoned / hot
süß	sweet
würzig	spicy

Worked example

READING

Tagesablauf
Lies Samiras Essensblog.

Frühstück: Gestern habe ich ein Brötchen mit Aufschnitt und ein Stück Obst dazu gegessen. Gestern war das ein Apfel, aber es kann auch eine Orange oder eine Birne sein.

Mittagessen: Das ist die Hauptmahlzeit, und ich esse immer einen Braten oder einen Hamburger mit Kartoffeln. Ich esse nie Fisch, weil mir der nicht schmeckt.

Abendessen: Das ist ein leichtes Essen und normalerweise esse ich eine Suppe oder ein Spiegelei. Ab und zu kommt auch ein Salat aufs Menü.

Kaffee und Kuchen: Während der Woche trinke ich meistens nur Mineralwasser, aber am Wochenende trinke ich gern eine heiße Schokolade oder eine Tasse Kräutertee und esse ein Stück Kuchen dazu. Letzten Sonntag habe ich eine Dose Limonade zu einem großen Stück Torte getrunken, weil ich Geburtstag hatte!

Was hat Samira wann gegessen? Trage entweder **Frühstück**, **Mittagessen**, **Abendessen** oder **Kaffee und Kuchen** ein.
Beispiel: Samira hat gestern zum Frühstück. einen Apfel gegessen.

Expanding your vocabulary

✓ While you are revising, keep expanding your vocabulary. All the words in this activity are ones which may crop up in an exam, so use an online dictionary to check their meanings and add them to your wordlists.

✓ Use the audioscripts from this book as well as the reading passages to find new words to learn – make a note of ones you think are useful and revise them for your writing and speaking tasks.

Now try this

READING

Now read Samira's food blog again and complete the activity.
(a) Samira hat Obst zum …… gegessen. **(1 mark)**
(b) Samira hat zum …… etwas Süßes getrunken. **(1 mark)**
(c) Manchmal isst Samira Tomaten und Gurke zum …… **(1 mark)**
(d) Samira isst immer Fleisch zum …… **(1 mark)**
(e) Wochentags isst Samira nichts zum …… **(1 mark)**

Food and drink

What is your favourite dish (Lieblingsessen)? Make sure you know how to say it in German.
See page 115 for lots of Obst and Gemüse vocabulary!

Essen

Braten (m)	roast
Ente (f)	duck
Hackfleisch (n)	mince
Käse (m)	cheese
Lammfleisch (n)	lamb
Leberwurst (f)	liver sausage
Obsttorte (f)	fruit pie
Pizza (f)	pizza
Reis (m)	rice
Schweinefleisch (n)	pork
Soße (f)	sauce
Spiegelei (n)	fried egg
Steak (n)	steak
Thunfisch (m)	tuna

Trinken

Bier (n)	beer
Fruchtsaft (m)	fruit juice
Limonade (f)	lemonade
Milch (f)	milk
Mineralwasser (n)	mineral water
Wein (m)	wine

Quantities

Be careful not to use von (of) with quantities:

eine Dose + Erbsen =

a tin of peas

Here are a few more:

ein Dutzend	a dozen
ein Glas	a jar / glass of
eine Packung	a packet of
eine Scheibe	a slice of
eine Tafel	a bar of
eine Tüte	a bag of

Wir essen gern Kuchen!
We like eating cake!

Developing a sentence

Start small: Ich esse gern Kekse.
Expand with und: Ich esse gern Kekse und Torten.
Double with a reason: Ich esse gern Kekse und Torten, weil sie mir so gut schmecken.

Worked example

Essen
Dein Austauschpartner Detlef schickt dir Fragen über deine Essgewohnheiten.
Schreibe eine Antwort an Detlef.
Du **musst** diese Punkte einschließen:
• was du nicht gern isst und warum
• was du gestern gegessen hast
• was du zum Frühstück gern isst
• ob du bei ihm Fastfood essen wirst.
Schreibe ungefähr 80–90 Wörter **auf Deutsch**.

(20 marks)

Ich esse nicht so gern Teigwaren mit Tomatensoße, weil sie mir nicht schmeckt. Ich esse lieber eine Fleischsoße. Mein Lieblingsessen ist Schinkenpizza ohne Käse, aber ich esse nicht gern indisches Essen, weil das zu würzig und scharf ist.

Present, past and future are all in these bullet points, so make sure you use these tenses yourself as you work your way through each point.

Expand your writing using **weil**, **und** and **aber**, like this student has done in the answer to the first bullet point: three easy steps to developing a sentence!

Now try this

Now write 80–90 words **in German** to answer the points above and complete the writing activity.

Shopping for clothes

Learn clothes with their **gender**, so you can make sure your adjectives agree.

Einkäufe

Auswahl (f)	choice
Geld (n)	money
Größe (f)	size
Kunde (m) / Kundin (f)	customer
Marke (f)	brand
Quittung (f)	receipt
Umkleidekabine (f)	changing room
anprobieren	to try on
umtauschen	to exchange
das passt / steht dir	that fits / that suits you

Kleider / Klamotten

Badeanzug (m)	swimming costume
Badehose (f)	trunks
Gürtel (m)	belt
Handschuh (m)	glove
Jeans (f)	jeans
Mütze (f)	cap
Schlafanzug (m)	pyjamas
Stiefel (m)	boot
altmodisch	old-fashioned
eng	tight
groß / weit	loose (i.e. too big)
mittelgroß	medium
schick / gepflegt / flott	smart

Adjective endings (der, die, das)

Masculine nouns

nom	acc	dat	
der blaue	den blauen	dem blauen	Mantel Pullover

Feminine nouns

nom / acc	dat	
die blaue	der blauen	Hose Jacke

Neuter nouns

nom / acc	dat	
das blaue	dem blauen	Hemd Kleid

Plural nouns

nom / acc	dat
die blauen Schuhe Socken	den blauen Schuhen Socken

Leder leather   Baumwolle cotton   Wolle wool

gepunktet spotted   gestreift striped   gefärbt dyed

Worked example

Instructions to candidate: You are exchanging an item at a clothes shop in Austria. Your teacher will play the role of the shop assistant and will speak first.

Task
Du bist im Kaufhaus in der Kleiderabteilung.
Du willst ein Kleidungsstück umtauschen.

1 Kleidungsstück und Problem
– Wie kann ich Ihnen helfen?
– Ich möchte bitte dieses Hemd umtauschen, weil es zu eng ist.

2 Feier
– Schade! Es ist so schön. Ist es für eine Party?
– Ja, für meinen Geburtstag.

3 !
– Wann haben Sie das gekauft?
– Ich habe es gestern gekauft.

In the Higher task you have one unexpected question to respond to. Make sure you mirror the tense in your answer.

Exam alert

When you read the instructions, decide what you are going to choose (in this case an item of clothing), check you know its gender and stick with that item. You do not have time to change your ideas once your preparation time is up.

This student has communicated both the item and the problem, just as was asked on the task card.

Now try this

Now practise the whole role play yourself, including the final two prompts:

4 ? Anderes Kleidungsstück

5 ? Preis

Listen to the recording

Social media

Be aware of separable verbs in listening and reading passages – the verb is not complete until you have heard / read the **whole** sentence to see if there is a missing prefix at the end!

Soziale Netzwerke

Blog (m/n)	blog
Chatraum (m)	chatroom
Homepage (f)	homepage
Internetseite / Webseite (f)	website
soziales Netzwerk (n)	social network
brennen	to burn
chatten	to chat (online)
hochladen	to upload
laden	to load
löschen	to delete
mailen	to email
sichern / speichern	to save
teilen	to share
tippen	to type

Separable verbs

Grammar page 96

Separable verbs break into two parts:
• main verb = second in the sentence
• prefix = at the end.
Make sure you can use separable verbs in all tenses.

hochladen – to upload
Present	Ich lade Fotos hoch.
Past	Ich habe Fotos hochgeladen.
Future	Ich werde Fotos hochladen.
Modals	Ich kann Fotos hochladen.

More separable verbs

ausschalten	to turn off
einschalten	to turn on
herunterladen	to download

Worked example

LISTENING TRACK 9

Technology

You hear an interview on the school radio.

What does it say?

Listen to the recording and put a cross ✗ in the correct box.

Listen to the recording

Example: ☒ The report is about social media.

☐ **A** 89% of teenagers had a profile.

☐ **B** All teenagers visit social media daily.

☐ **C** Gerd enjoys uploading content to his social media pages.

☐ **D** He finds commenting on other people's content fun.

☐ **E** Gerd never posts online.

☐ **F** Gerd shares digital material online.

– Diese Woche diskutieren wir im Schulradio: Jugendliche und soziale Medien.

Hilfe! Die Katze hat mein Profil gelöscht!
Help! The cat has deleted my profile!

Exam alert

Numbers are bound to come up somewhere in the exams, so make sure you are confident with them – see page 108 to brush up on them now.

Use the example answer to help you settle into the listening activity.

Now try this

LISTENING TRACK 10

Now listen to the rest of the recording and put a cross next to the **three** remaining correct statements. **(3 marks)**

Listen to the recording

Listen carefully to **every** word – Gerd says **manche Jugendliche** (some teenagers). That is not statement **B** (all teenagers).

Technology

In the Speaking exam, you could be asked about what technology you use and the effect it has on your life – be prepared with the vocabulary on this page!

Technologie

Anschluss (m) / Verbindung (f)	connection
E-Mail (f)	email
Handy (n)	mobile phone
Passwort (n)	password
Platte (f)	disk
Schrägstrich (m)	forward slash
Smartphone (n)	smartphone
Software (f)	software
Tablet-PC (m)	tablet computer
Telefon (n)	telephone
Webcam / Netzkamera (f)	webcam
(be)nutzen	to use
digital	digital

Pluperfect tense

Grammar page 105

Pluperfect tense = had done something.
It is formed by using the imperfect form of haben / sein + past participle.

Ich hatte es gedruckt.   I had printed it.
Sie war online gewesen.   She had been online.

Bildschirm (m) screen   Drucker (m) printer
Tastatur (f) keyboard   Taste (f) key   Computer (m) computer

Worked example

Technology

Beantworte diese Frage:

- Wie benutzt du Technologie zu Hause?

> Abends sehe ich gern meine Lieblingsserien auf meinem Tablet-PC. Im Moment spare ich mein Taschengeld, um ein Smartphone zu kaufen, weil ich das echt super finde.

Aiming higher

> Zu Hause werden wir in Zukunft immer mehr Technologie haben, denke ich. Abends sitzen wir im Wohnzimmer zusammen und jeder sieht schon seinen eigenen Bildschirm an. Das finde ich schade, weil wir uns nicht direkt miteinander unterhalten. Letzten Monat hat meine Mutter mir einen neuen Computer für die Schulaufgaben gekauft und ich finde ihn sehr nützlich.

A solid piece of writing – starting both sentences with time phrases – makes this work flow nicely and the **um ... zu** clause shows good command of the German language. Note also the opinion used.

Adapting tenses

Prepare to speak in a variety of tenses by imagining that the question is in the past tense (Wie hast du letzte Woche Technologie zu Hause benutzt?) or in the future tense (Wie wirst du in Zukunft Technologie benutzen?).

You can use the same vocabulary, but you just need to change the tense each time to suit the question being asked.

This student uses:
- **wir** and **ich** parts of the verb
- **jeder** (everyone) + **sieht**
- an idiom: **schade** (pity)
- a reflexive verb: **sich unterhalten**
- present, past and future tenses

The length of time you speak for is crucial. Don't try to squeeze too much content in – you might run out of time. it is important that your conversation flows and that you speak clearly and don't gabble.

Now try this

Now prepare to speak for about 30 seconds on the same subject.

Wie benutzt du Technologie zu Hause?

Online activities

Use time phrases – zu oft, fast täglich, kaum – to add interest when discussing your online life.

Aktivitäten online

Ich spiele online / Computerspiele.	I play online / computer games.
Ich lade Fotos hoch.	I upload photos.
Ich lade Musik herunter.	I download music.
Ich sehe mir Videoclips an.	I watch video clips.
Ich surfe im Internet.	I surf the internet.
Ich schreibe E-Mails / mein Blog.	I write emails / my blog.
Ich chatte online mit meinen Freunden.	I chat to my friends online.
Ich besuche Chatrooms.	I visit chatrooms.
Ich benutze soziale Netzwerke.	I use social networking sites.
Ich bleibe mit meinen Freunden in Kontakt.	I stay in contact with my friends.
Ich mache Einkäufe.	I do shopping.
Ich schicke eine Kurznachricht. / Ich simse.	I send a text.
Ich lese die Nachrichten am Computer.	I read the news on the computer.

Dürfen (to be allowed to)

Grammar page 98

Dürfen is a modal verb so it needs an infinitive.
Ich darf nicht nach 22:00 Uhr auf Facebook surfen.
I am not allowed to be on Facebook after ten o'clock.
Ich darf keine Musik herunterladen.
I am not allowed to download music.

Worked example

 LISTENING TRACK 11

Daily life

You hear this podcast about a teenager's life. Listen to the recording and answer the following question **in English**.

Listen to the recording

(a) Why does Mia look forward to the evening? **(1 mark)**

she can relax

— Mia freut sich immer auf den Abend, weil sie sich dann endlich einmal ausruhen kann.

Listening tips

✓ Don't worry about doing a simultaneous translation for yourself as you listen – read the questions in advance and then focus on the parts of the recording that are **relevant** to those questions.

✓ The more practice you have of **listening** to German, the easier you will find it. Make sure you listen to all the recorded material supplied with this Revision Guide to give your listening skills a boost.

Now try this

Listen to the recording **LISTENING TRACK 12**

Now listen to the rest of the recording and answer the following questions **in English**.

(b) Why does Mia have to watch the news? **(1 mark)**
(c) What does Mia do when she phones her friends? **(1 mark)**
(d) Give **two** actions Mia does after she has phoned her friends. **(2 marks)**
(e) Why does Mia feel nervous? **(1 mark)**

There are several cognates (words similar to English words) in this recording – use them to help you understand.

For and against technology

Be prepared to give positive and negative views on modern technology by using the phrases here.

Technologie: für und gegen

Computerspiele sind kreativ.
Computer games are creative.

Man kann in Kontakt mit Leuten aus der ganzen Welt bleiben.

You can stay in contact with people from all over the world.

Die Spiele sind lehrreich.
The games are educational.

Man muss sich der Gefahren bewusst sein.
You must be aware of the dangers.

Computerspiele sind eine Geld- und Zeitverschwendung.

Computer games are a waste of money and time.

Bildschirme sind für die Augen schädlich.
Screens are damaging for the eyes.

Internet-Mobbing ist ein großes Problem für Jugendliche.

Cyberbullying is a big problem for teenagers.

Es gibt immer ein Risiko mit Online-Aktivitäten.
There is always a risk with online activities.

Für junge Kinder ist das Internet zu gefährlich.
The internet is too dangerous for young children.

Using ob (whether)

Grammar page 93

Ob sends the verb to the end:

Ich weiß nicht, ob er online ist.
I don't know whether he is online.

These conjunctions all send the verb to the end of the clause too:

als	when (in the past)
dass	that
obwohl	although
wenn	if

Als ich ein Kind war, hat das Internet mich fasziniert.

When I was a child, the internet fascinated me.

Aiming higher

✓ Use meiner Meinung nach + imperfect modal.

✓ A present tense modal reinforces knowledge of modal + infinitive.

✓ Use obwohl, which sends the verb to the end.

✓ Use higher level structures such as etwas anderes and sich vorstellen + dative pronoun.

Worked example

Technologie: Vor- und Nachteile

Schreibe einen Artikel für eine Technologiewebsite.
Du **musst** diesen Punkt einschließen:
• ob du Technologie eher positiv oder negativ findest.

Aiming higher

Meiner Meinung nach sollten die Eltern dafür verantwortlich sein, dass ihre Kinder sich körperlich betätigen und nicht das Risiko eingehen, computersüchtig zu werden. Obwohl ich mir ein Leben ohne Computer nicht vorstellen kann, weiß ich schon, wann die Bildschirmzeit zu Ende sein sollte und wann ich etwas anderes und Gesundes machen muss.

Once you have written your text, check that:

• **word order is correct** (verb second or sent to the end by subordinating conjunction)

• **tenses are secure** and make sense (don't hop from past to present to future without time markers or sensible meaning)

• **spelling is accurate**, including adjective endings, genders and capital letters.

Now try this

Now prepare answers to these points and complete the above writing activity:

• ob du Technologie eher positiv oder negativ findest
• wie dir Technologie besonders geholfen hat
• was du für junge Kinder im Bereich Technologie nicht empfehlen würdest
• ob du in Zukunft mit Technologie arbeiten wirst und warum (nicht).

Rechtfertige deine Ideen und Meinungen.
Schreibe ungefähr 130–150 Wörter **auf Deutsch**.

Don't forget to justify (rechtfertigen) your ideas – in other words, give a reason for the ideas and opinions you express!

Hobbies

Make sure you can talk about your hobbies, as well as those of family and friends, by learning the different parts of present tense verbs.

Hobbys

Ich sehe gern fern.

Ich spiele gern Computerspiele.

Ich höre gern Musik.

Ich koche gern.

Ich lese gern.

Ich spiele gern Schach.

Ich schicke gern SMS.

Ich gehe gern kegeln.

Ich treibe gern Sport.

Present tense (regular)

Grammar page 95

machen – **to do / to make**

ich	mache
du	machst
er / sie / es	macht
wir	machen
ihr	macht
Sie / sie	machen

infinitive

Gehen (to go) follows the same pattern as machen in the present tense.

Ich trainiere.
I do training.

Ich gehe gern aus.
I like going out.

Worked example

 LISTENING TRACK **13**

Leisure time

You hear a recording about leisure time. What do you find out?

Listen to the recording and complete the sentence by putting a cross ✗ in the correct box.

Example: In her free time, Anna enjoys …

☐ **A** shopping
☒ **B** cooking
☐ **C** going out
☐ **D** watching TV

— In meiner Freizeit bin ich oft in der Küche, weil ich sehr gern backe.

 Listen to the recording

- You are not necessarily going to hear the **exact** activity you are familiar with, but you will hear enough to lead you to the words you know.
- Anna says she is mostly **in der Küche**. **Küche** means kitchen, so select the phrase which is related to this.
- There is only one suitable answer here, which is **B** cooking. Nothing else is vaguely related to 'kitchen' or 'baking'.

 Listen to the recording

 LISTENING TRACK **14**

Now try this

Now listen to three more people saying what they enjoy doing and put a cross ✗ in the correct box.

(a) In the evenings, Oliver enjoys …
☐ **A** doing sport
☐ **B** cooking
☐ **C** going out
☐ **D** watching TV
(1 mark)

(b) Petra is always …
☐ **A** listening to music
☐ **B** meeting friends
☐ **C** studying
☐ **D** playing the piano
(1 mark)

(c) At the moment Bert is enjoying …
☐ **A** singing
☐ **B** writing
☐ **C** reading
☐ **D** playing sport
(1 mark)

Interests

Make sure you can say what you **do** and do **not** enjoy doing in your leisure time.

Interessen

Bergsteigen finde ich toll.	I find mountaineering great.
Als Hobby bevorzuge ich Bogenschießen.	As a hobby I prefer archery.
Meine Lieblingsfreizeitbeschäftigung ist Chillen.	My favourite leisure activity is chilling.
Ich sammle gern Karten.	I like collecting cards.
Ich gehe nachmittags in den Sportverein.	I go to the sports club in the afternoons.
Diese Unterhaltung finde ich prima.	I find this entertainment great.
Ich gehe gern mit dem Hund spazieren.	I like going for a walk with the dog.
Ich gebe mein Taschengeld für Musik aus.	I spend my pocket money on music.
Ich gehe lieber ins Kino als ins Konzert.	I prefer going to the cinema than to a concert.
An Klettern habe ich wenig Interesse.	I have little interest in climbing.
Das macht mir keinen Spaß.	I don't enjoy that.
Ich interessiere mich nicht für Nachtklubs.	I am not interested in nightclubs.

Weil (because)

> Grammar page 93

Weil **always** sends the verb to the **end**.

Ich kann nicht kommen, weil …
I can't come because …
  ich dann Fußballtraining mache.
  I've got football training then.
  ich kein Geld habe.
  I haven't got any money.
  meine Eltern es nicht erlauben.
  my parents won't allow it.
  Verwandte zu Besuch sind.
  relatives are visiting.

Haben and **sein** in the perfect tense go after the past participle.
Modal verbs go after the infinitive.

Ich kann nicht kommen, weil …
I can't come because …
  ich den Film schon gesehen habe.
  I have already seen the film.
  ich Hausaufgaben machen muss.
  I've got to do homework.

Worked example

Translation
Translate this passage **into English**.   **(3 marks)**

> Am Wochenende gehe ich immer in den Sportverein.
> Ich mache dort Fitnesstraining, oder ich spiele Federball.

At the weekend I always go to the sports club.
I do fitness training there or I play badminton.

Don't miss out any words in a translation, such as **dort** here – what does it tell you?

Learning vocabulary

To be able to translate into English, you need to recognise lots of vocabulary, so learning plenty is crucial to success.

☑ **Look** at and learn the German words.
☑ **Cover** the English words.
☑ **Write** the English words.
☑ **Look** at all the words.
☑ **See** how many you have got right.

To help prepare for the translation into German, cover the **German** words and repeat the above stages.

Now try this

Now complete the translation.

> Gestern bin ich mit meiner Familie ins Kino gegangen. Du würdest den Film langweilig finden, weil die Spezialeffekte altmodisch waren.

(4 marks)

Don't ignore the pronoun in this second sentence – **du**. Who is it referring to?

Music

Whether you love listening to music or prefer to play in an orchestra, it is important to know vocabulary about this topic.

Musik

ich spiele + instrument – no need for 'a'

Ich spiele ...   I play ...

 Flöte (f)

 Geige (f)

Gitarre (f)

Klarinette (n)

Klavier (n)

Schlagzeug (n)

Trompete (f)

Ich höre gern ...   I like listening to ...
Popmusik / Rockmusik (f) pop / rock music

Worked example

WRITING

Musik machen

Du postest dieses Foto online für deine Freunde.

Beschreibe das Foto und schreibe deine Meinung über Musik.

Schreibe ungefähr 20–30 Wörter **auf Deutsch**.
(12 marks)

In diesem Foto gibt es eine Band. Zwei Jungen spielen Gitarre und ein Jugendlicher singt. Ich höre gern Musik und ich bin Mitglied im Schulorchester. Musik ist wichtig für mich.

There are **two** parts to this writing task – a description of the photo **and** your opinion about music generally.

Favourite things

Use Lieblings + any noun (lower case) to talk about favourite things.

-band / -gruppe (f) group

-melodie (f) tune

Lieblings

-sänger (m)
-sängerin (f) singer

-lied (n) song

-orchester (n) orchestra

Now try this

WRITING

Now answer the photo question for yourself.

Remember, half your writing must be description and half opinion.

Sport

You may want to refer to sports when talking about various topics. Make sure the **main verb** always comes in **second** position in a sentence.

Sportarten

ich ...	I ...
angle	go fishing
jogge	go jogging
reite	go riding
fahre Rad	go cycling
fahre Skateboard	go skateboarding
gehe schwimmen	go swimming
mache Gymnastik	do gymnastics
mache Leichtathletik	do athletics
laufe Rollschuh	go rollerskating
spiele Fußball	play football
spiele Tischtennis	play table tennis
treibe Sport	do sport

Ich bin Mitglied einer Hockeymannschaft.
I am a member of a hockey team.

Letzte Saison haben wir die Meisterschaft gewonnen.
We won the championship last season.

Verb in second place

Grammar page 92

1 Ich **2** spiele **3** Rugby.

1 Im Winter **2** spiele **3** ich **4** Rugby.

In the perfect tense, the part of haben or sein goes in second place.

1 Im Winter **2** habe **3** ich **4** Rugby **5** gespielt.

Im Sommer spiele ich Tennis.

Worked example

 SPEAKING

Sports activities

Beantworte diese Frage:

- Welche Sportarten treibst du gern?

 Aiming higher

Ich bin sehr aktiv und treibe dreimal in der Woche Sport. Letztes Jahr war es ganz anders, weil ich mir das Bein gebrochen hatte und vier Monate lang keinen Sport treiben konnte. Das war eine Katastrophe für mich und ich musste dauernd Computerspiele spielen, die ich langweilig fand. Mein Traum ist es, eines Tages Profifußballer zu werden und ich würde am allerliebsten für Chelsea spielen.

Aiming higher

Including three tenses in your work is as easy as 1, 2, 3, if you can say which sports you:

- ✓ **do** now
- ✓ **did** previously
- ✓ **would like to do** or **will do**.

Use past tense 'markers' such as **letztes Jahr** (last year), **in der vorigen Saison** (last season), **eines Tages** (one day).

Now try this

 SPEAKING

Now prepare to answer these questions as fully as you can:

- Welche Sportarten treibst du gern?
- Wie viel Sport hast du letzte Woche gemacht?
- Was wäre dein sportlicher Traum?
- Soll Sport in der Schule Pflicht sein?

Try to speak for at least 30 seconds on each point.

Here's a useful Higher level phrase:

Mein Traum ist es, mein Land bei den Olympischen Spielen zu vertreten. It is my dream to represent my country at the Olympic Games.

Reading

Reading is something exam boards enjoy promoting, so make sure you are not caught out by this topic!

Lesen

Comic (m) / Comicheft (n)   Krimi (m)   Roman (m)

Schauspiel (n)   Zeitschrift (f)   Zeitung (f)

Imperfect tense

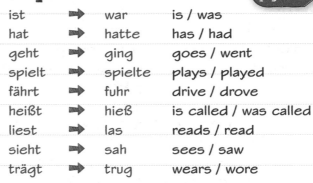
Grammar page 102

ist ➡	war	is / was
hat ➡	hatte	has / had
geht ➡	ging	goes / went
spielt ➡	spielte	plays / played
fährt ➡	fuhr	drive / drove
heißt ➡	hieß	is called / was called
liest ➡	las	reads / read
sieht ➡	sah	sees / saw
trägt ➡	trug	wears / wore

Im Buch ging es um Freiheit / einen Mord / eine Beziehung.

The book was about freedom / a murder / a relationship.

Worked example

Paula die Leseratte by **Martin Ebbertz**

Read the extract from the text.

Paula is being introduced to the reader.

> Es war einmal eine Leseratte, die hieß Paula und die trug eine große Brille mit dicken Gläsern. Die Gläser waren so dick, dass es aussah, als hätte Paula winzige Augen. … Ohne Brille sah Paula überhaupt nichts, und mit Brille sah sie zwar ein bisschen, doch immer noch sehr wenig. Und das ist für eine Leseratte schlecht, denn zum Lesen braucht man gute Augen. Paula sah so wenig, und das Lesen war für sie so anstrengend, dass sie an jedem Tag nur einen Buchstaben las.

Answer the following question **in English**.

(a) How can you tell Paula was short-sighted? **(1 mark)**

She wore thick glasses / had thick lenses in her glasses.

Now try this

Now answer these three further questions on the extract **in English**.
You do not need to write in full sentences.

(b) What effect did Paula's glasses have on her eyes? **(1 mark)**

(c) What could Paula see without her glasses? **(1 mark)**

(d) Give **two** reasons why Paula made slow progress with her reading. **(2 marks)**

Films

Films, books and television programmes all require the same kind of vocabulary, so make sure you are secure with the basics, and then transfer them across these topics.

Kino

fantastisch	fantastic
komisch	funny (strange)
spannend	exciting
toll	great
traurig	sad

Ich habe ... im Kino / auf DVD gesehen.
I saw ... at the cinema / on DVD.

Es war ein Abenteuerfilm / Horrorfilm / Liebesfilm.
It was an adventure / horror / love film.

Das Hauptthema war Liebe / Familie.
The main theme was love / family.

Die Geschichte war kompliziert / romantisch.
The story was complicated / romantic.

Der Film spielte in Köln. The film was set in Cologne.

Time expressions

Add time expressions wherever you can.

ab und zu	now and again
dann und wann	now and then
immer	always
manchmal	sometimes
nie	never
oft	often
selten	seldom

These sentences both mean the same thing, but have a different word order!

Ich gehe manchmal ins Kino.
Manchmal gehe ich ins Kino.
I sometimes go to the cinema.

Worked example

Ein Filmfest
Du organisierst ein Filmfest für Jugendliche in deiner Stadt.

Schreibe einen offiziellen Brief an die österreichische Partnerschule, damit die Schüler zum Filmfest kommen, wenn sie zu Besuch sind.

Du **musst** diese Punkte einschließen:

• Details zum Filmfest
• warum die Austauschschüler zum Fest kommen sollten
• wie das Filmfest letztes Jahr gelaufen ist
• warum das Fest dieses Jahr besser sein wird.

Rechtfertige deine Ideen und Meinungen.

Schreibe ungefähr 130–150 Wörter **auf Deutsch**.

(28 marks)

Sehr geehrte Frau Bach,

ich möchte Sie heute über ein Filmfest informieren, das ich und meine Mitschüler organisieren. Das Fest heißt „Kino lebt" und es wird in der Woche vom 12. bis zum 19. Mai hier an der Schule stattfinden.

Writing tips

Read the rubric.

✓ **Who** are you addressing? Is your writing for a Sie or a du person?

✓ **What** are you writing? A letter, a report or a blog?

✓ **Make notes** beside each bullet point to focus your mind before you start writing – do not go off message.

✓ Keep an eye on **tenses** – include a good variety across the bullet points.

✓ Be decisive – **plan** an answer and **stick** to it!

This paragraph is 40 words in length, so the student must move on to address the remaining three bullet points to complete the task. Look how the student has already worked in the present and future tenses!

Now try this

Now prepare your own answers to the bullet points on the left and complete the writing activity.

Can you come in on target?

Television

When reading or listening to extracts, tense markers such as those below can all help you identify when the action is happening.

Fernsehsendungen

Ich sehe mir gern … an.	I like watching …
Dokumentarfilm (m)	documentary
Fernsehstar (m)	TV celebrity
Kabelfernsehen (n)	cable TV
Lieblingsprogramm (n)	favourite programme
die Nachrichten (pl)	the news
Quizsendung (f)	quiz programme
Seifenoper (f)	soap opera
Sendung (f)	(TV) programme
Serie (f)	series
Show (f)	show
Zeichentrickfilme (mpl)	cartoons
Zuschauer/in (m/f)	viewer
einschalten	to switch on
ausschalten	to switch off

ZDF and ARD are TV broadcasters.

Tense markers

Past tense

als kleines Kind	as a small child
früher	previously, in the past
gestern	yesterday
letzte Woche	last week

Present tense

heute	today
heutzutage	these days
jetzt	now
momentan	at the moment

Future tense

in Zukunft	in future
morgen (früh)	tomorrow (morning)
nächste Woche	next week
übermorgen	the day after tomorrow

Ich sehe mir gern Zeichentrickfilme an.

Worked example

LISTENING TRACK 15

Podcast
Du hörst einen Podcast im Internet über Sophies Freizeit.

Was sagt sie? Trage entweder **entspannend, interessant, blöd** oder **lustig** ein. Du kannst jedes Wort mehr als einmal verwenden.

Beispiel: Sophie findet Musiksendungen
<u>entspannend</u>

> — Normalerweise schalte ich nach der Schule den Fernseher ein und sehe mir eine Musiksendung an, um mich auszuruhen.

- Read the **four** adjectives carefully and make sure you know what they mean.
- Don't mistake **entspannend** (relaxing) for **spannend** (exciting) here.
- A process of elimination can help you in this sort of activity – if you are not sure which is the correct adjective, it may be helpful to narrow your options by ruling out some of the adjectives first.
- Copy the whole adjective into the space provided – abbreviations or translations are not what are asked for here!

Now try this

LISTENING TRACK 16

Listen to the rest of the recording and complete the sentences.
(a) Als Kind hat Sophie Zeichentrickfilme ……………………… gefunden. **(1 mark)**
(b) Jetzt findet sie die Zeichentrickfilme ……………………… . **(1 mark)**
(c) Sophie hat Dokumentarfilme ……………………… gefunden. **(1 mark)**
(d) Sophie findet die Nachrichten gar nicht ……………………… . **(1 mark)**
(e) Sophie mag Filme, die ……………………… sind. **(1 mark)**

Celebrations

Prepare yourself to talk about parties and celebrations with the vocabulary on this page.

Feier

Ehe (f)	marriage
Feuerwerk (n)	fireworks
Herzlichen Glückwunsch zum Geburtstag!	Happy Birthday!
Hochzeit (f)	wedding
Hochzeitsfeier (f)	wedding celebration
Sekt (m)	sparkling wine
Spezialität (f)	speciality
Torte (f)	gateau
Verlobung (f)	engagement
feiern	to celebrate
sich verkleiden	to dress up (costume)

Dative prepositions

Grammar page 86

aus	from	nach	after
außer	except	seit	since
bei	at (the home of)	von	from
mit	with	zu	to

(m) der Freund ➡ bei dem Freund
at the friend's house

(f) die Party ➡ nach der Party
after the party

(n) das Zimmer ➡ aus dem Zimmer
out of the room

(pl) die Geschenke ➡ mit den Geschenken
with the gifts

Frohes Neues Jahr!
Happy New Year!

zu + dem = zum
zu + der = zur
von + dem = vom

Worked example

READING

Celebrations
Read this blog post by Alex.

> Wir feiern immer zum Geburtstag als Familie. Meine Schwester backt meine Lieblingsschokoladentorte. Mein Bruder kauft oft die Luftballons. Meine Oma schickt mir immer Geld in der Post und mein Opa trinkt ein Glas Sekt für mich!
>
> Ich gehe aber nie ins Büro, weil man das an so einem besonderen Tag nicht machen soll!

Complete the gap in each sentence using a word from the box below. There are more words than gaps.

Example: Alex is writing about a ...~~birthday~~...

mobile phone   never   money   ~~birthday~~   cake   often
wedding   eats   card   drinks   always   works

Exam alert

In this style of activity, there are often **two** answers which could fit each gap grammatically, so use your knowledge and understanding of the text to lead you to the correct word.

You need a noun for this gap – so ignore the time expressions and the verbs.

Now try this

READING

Now complete the above reading activity.
(a) His sister makes a ....   **(1 mark)**
(b) His brother .... buys balloons.   **(1 mark)**
(c) He receives .... in the post.   **(1 mark)**
(d) His grandad .... something special.   **(1 mark)**
(e) Alex never .... on his special day. **(1 mark)**

Festivals

Festival vocabulary could come up in any part of your exams – make sure these words don't throw you!

Feste

Muttertag (m)

Ostern (n)

Silvester (n)

Weihnachten (n)

Fasching (m) / Karneval (m)

Dorffest (n)

Dreikönigsfest (n)	Epiphany (6 January)
Fastenzeit (f)	Lent
Heiligabend (m)	Christmas Eve
Karfreitag (m)	Good Friday
Ostermontag (m)	Easter Monday
Glühwein (m)	punch
Imbissstube (f)	snack bar
Krapfen (m)	doughnut
Umzug (m)	procession
Volksmusik (f)	folk music

Accusative prepositions

Grammar page 86

The following prepositions are followed by the accusative case:

durch	through
ohne	without
für	for
um	around
gegen	against / towards

- (m) der Bruder ➡ für den Bruder
  (der ➡ den) for the brother
- (f) die Idee ➡ gegen die Idee
  against the idea
- (n) das Haus ➡ um das Haus
  around the house
- (pl) die Getränke ➡ ohne die Getränke
  without the drinks

zu Weihnachten – at Christmas
an Neujahr – at New Year
auf der Neujahrsparty – at the New Year's party

Worked example

WRITING

Feiern
Übersetze **ins Deutsche**.

At Christmas I will take part in the procession through the town, because I like to dress up.

Zu Weihnachten werde ich am Umzug durch die Stadt teilnehmen, weil ich mich gern verkleide.

Aiming higher

- ✓ Get your word order right by reminding yourself of the rule: **time – manner – place**. Which is which in this first sentence?
- ✓ If you use a weil clause, make sure you send the following verb to the end: weil ich mich gern verkleide.

Now try this

WRITING

Now complete the translation **into German**.

When my boyfriend had a carnival party, I did not enjoy it at all and I went home early. This year I will go into the town centre for New Year's Eve, because there will be a band on the market square and we can dance there. I would like most of all to celebrate with a large crowd outside.

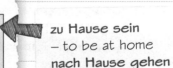

zu Hause sein
– to be at home
nach Hause gehen
– to go home

Holiday preferences

What sort of holiday do you like – sporty, lazy, chilled? As well as saying what you **do** enjoy doing, make sure you can say what you **don't** enjoy.

Thinking positively

Ich mache gern Urlaub in (Amerika).
I like going on holiday to (America).

Ich ziehe (Aktivurlaube) vor.
I prefer (active holidays).

Am liebsten (bleibe ich in einem Hotel).
Most of all I like (staying in a hotel).

Mein Lieblingsurlaub wäre (eine Woche in der Türkei).
My favourite holiday would be (a week in Turkey).

Urlaub mit Freunden finde ich …	I find holidays with friends …
ausgezeichnet.	excellent.
entspannend.	relaxing.
locker.	relaxed / chilled.
super / prima.	super.

Thinking negatively

Ich fahre nicht gern (ins Ausland).
I don't like going (abroad).

(Sporturlaube) kann ich nicht ausstehen.
I can't stand (sports holidays).

Ich würde nie (Skiurlaub machen).
I would never (go on a skiing holiday).

(Eine Woche in der Sonne) interessiert mich nicht.
(A week in the sun) doesn't interest me.

Es gefällt mir gar nicht, (die Sehenswürdigkeiten zu besuchen).
I don't like (visiting the sights) at all.

Familienurlaub finde ich …	I find family holidays …
ermüdend.	tiring.
schlecht.	bad.
schrecklich.	terrible.
stressig.	stressful.

Worked example

Ein idealer Urlaub

Deine Freundin schickt dir Fragen über deinen idealen Urlaub. Schreibe eine Antwort.

Du **musst** diesen Punkt einschließen:

• wohin du gern in den Urlaub fährst.

> Ich fahre in den Ferien sehr gern ans Meer. Ich bin Wassersportfan. Ich windsurfe gern. Ich liebe Segeln.

Skiurlaube interessieren mich nicht.

Although this is an accurate answer, it does little to show Higher skills because the sentences are very short and basic.

Aiming higher

> In den Sommerferien fahre ich sehr gern ans Meer, da ich ein ziemlich großer Wassersportfan bin. Ich windsurfe äußerst gern, aber am liebsten segele ich. Segeln ist meine Leidenschaft.

To improve your writing:
• Add more detail, which this student does by using **Sommer** + **ferien**.
• Add an adjective.
• Include a **da** (because, since) or **weil** clause – with verb to the end!
• Add **am liebsten** to express preference.
• Combine your sentences with the connective **aber**.

Now try this

Now include these points and complete the above writing activity:
• was du im letzten Urlaub gemacht hast
• wie du das gefunden hast
• warum ein Urlaub wichtig ist oder nicht
• Pläne für den nächsten Urlaub.

Schreibe ungefähr 80–90 Wörter **auf Deutsch**.

Hotels

Much of the hotel vocabulary on this page is also relevant for staying at a bed and breakfast or a youth hostel.

Im Hotel wohnen

Aufenthaltsraum (m)	games room
Aufzug / Fahrstuhl (m)	lift
Fenster (n)	window
Fitnessraum (m)	gym
Gast (m)	guest
Gepäck (n)	luggage
Klimaanlage (f)	air conditioning
Koffer (m)	suitcase
Reservierung (f)	reservation
Satellitenfernsehen (n)	satellite TV
Schwimmbad (n)	pool
auspacken	to unpack
funktionieren	to work
familienfreundlich	family friendly
mit Blick auf	with a view of

Compound words

Germans love long words! If you are joining words together in the Writing or Speaking exam to make a new word, the gender of the word is determined by the last word in the compound noun.

das Spiel + der Platz = **der** Spielplatz
(playground)

der Preis + die Liste = **die** Preisliste (price list)

die Stadt + das Zentrum = **das** Stadtzentrum
(town centre)

die Unterhaltung + die Möglichkeiten =
 die Unterhaltungsmöglichkeiten (things to do)

If you come across a long word in a reading extract, take it apart, as above, to work out what each part means individually.

Worked example

Ein Hotelbesuch

Lies Ninas Blogpost.

Unser Hotel bietet viele Unterhaltungsmöglichkeiten.

Die Familienreise im Frühling macht immer viel Spaß. Das ist ein absoluter Höhepunkt für mich! Wir wohnen in einem Drei-Sterne-Hotel. Das Hotel hat einen Fitnessraum, ein Schwimmbad und ein tolles Abendunterhaltungsprogramm. Glücklicherweise hat jedes Zimmer Anschluss zum Internet. Mein jüngerer Bruder kann sich gut selbst unterhalten. Am Ende des Aufenthalts versprechen wir, dieselben Zimmer für das folgende Jahr zu reservieren. Es ist immer ein einmaliger Urlaub!

Exam alert

In this style of activity, you have to understand **both** the extract itself **and** the questions. Break down the long words to help you understand the extract **before** you tackle the questions, one by one.

Fülle die Lücke in diesem Satz mit einem Wort aus dem Kasten.

Beispiel: Nina findet die Frühlingsreise wunderbar

Bett	schwimmen	viel	regelmäßig	plant	~~wunderbar~~
reserviert	online	selten	Zelt	langweilig	nichts

You won't find the exact sentence from the extract in the questions – you need to understand the meaning of the extract to choose the correct answer.

Now try this

Now complete the above reading activity.

(a)	Nina schläft in einem	**(1 mark)**
(b)	Abends gibt es .... zu tun.	**(1 mark)**
(c)	Ninas Bruder geht gern	**(1 mark)**
(d)	Ninas Familie bleibt .... hier.	**(1 mark)**
(e)	Sie .... schon den nächsten Urlaub.	**(1 mark)**

You won't need to use all the words from the box.

Es gibt mehr Wörter als Lücken.

Campsites

Most of the vocabulary for this topic will also be useful for other types of holiday accommodation.

Auf dem Campingplatz

Badetuch (n)	towel
Bettwäsche (f)	bedlinen
Grill (m)	barbecue
Schlafsack (m)	sleeping bag
Wanderweg (m)	walk / trail
Zahnbürste (f)	toothbrush
Zahnpasta (f)	toothpaste
buchen	to book
reservieren	to reserve
wandern	to walk / hike
zelten	to camp
im Freien	in the open air
im Wohnwagen (m)	in a caravan
im Zelt (n)	in a tent

Giving location details

Here are some ways of letting someone know where you live or are staying.

am	at / on
dort	there
entfernt	away from
hier	here
in der Nähe von	near to
neben	next to

Der Campingplatz ...	The campsite ...
liegt in der Nähe von Lindau.	is near to Lindau.
ist etwa 30 Gehminuten vom Stadtzentrum entfernt.	is about 30 minutes on foot from the town centre.
liegt am Bodensee.	is on Lake Constance.
befindet sich am Waldrand.	is situated on the edge of the wood.

Unser Campingplatz befindet sich direkt am Meer.

Worked example

Campsite

You hear this campsite advertisement on local radio in Germany. What do you find out?

Listen to the recording and put a cross ✗ next to the correct statement.

Example: ☒ You can hire a boat.

☐ **A** The campsite is looking for a new manager.

☐ **B** You can hire a tent.

☐ **C** Caravans are allowed on site.

☐ **D** You cannot reserve a pitch.

☐ **E** The campsite is divided into four areas.

☐ **F** You have to bring your own drinking water.

☐ **G** There will be a new area for washing.

— Herzlich willkommen auf dem Campingplatz Maria am Bodensee. Neu ist dieses Jahr unser Bootsverleih (Kajak und Kanu) vor Ort.

Bodensee – Lake Constance

- Identify language which is not needed for the question. Here, the first couple of words are 'padding' and can be ignored. They don't offer any information about the campsite.
- Use all the clues provided. Don't be worried by **Bootsverleih** when you hear it mentioned. The cognates **Boot**, **Kajak** and **Kanu** along with the context of a campsite on Lake Constance should lead you to its meaning: boat hire.

Now try this

Now listen to the rest of the recording and put a cross next to each of the other **three** correct statements.

(3 marks)

Accommodation

Use this page to help you say what type of holiday accommodation you prefer.

Die Ferienunterkunft

Bauernhaus (n)	farmhouse
Bauernhof (m)	farm
Campingplatz (m)	campsite
Ferienwohnung (f)	holiday flat
Halbpension (f)	half board
Hotel (n)	hotel
Jugendherberge (f)	youth hostel
Mietwohnung (f)	rented flat
Pension (f)	bed and breakfast place
Übernachtung (f)	overnight stay
Unterkunft (f)	accommodation
Wohnwagen (m)	caravan, mobile home
mieten	to hire, rent
übernachten	to stay the night
im Voraus	in advance
inbegriffen	included

Gern, lieber, am liebsten

A simple way of showing a preference is to use gern (like), lieber (prefer) and am liebsten (like most of all).

gern ♥
lieber ♥♥
am liebsten ♥♥♥

- Put gern and lieber after the verb:
  Ich schlafe gern im Freien.
  I like sleeping outdoors.
  Ich bleibe lieber im Hotel.
  I prefer staying in a hotel.

- Use am liebsten to start your sentence:
  Am liebsten zelte ich.
  Most of all I like camping.

Ich schlafe lieber im Freien.

Worked example

Holidays and travel

Beantworte diese Frage:

- Wo übernachtest du am liebsten im Urlaub?

Aiming higher

Letzten Sommer haben wir in einer Pension übernachtet, aber das war schrecklich, weil wir abends um neun Uhr ins Bett gehen mussten. Diesen Sommer werden wir eine Ferienwohnung mieten und ich freue mich darauf.
Ich finde es ungemütlich, im Zelt zu schlafen, weil es oft so kalt und unbequem ist. Am liebsten übernachte ich in einem Hotel.

Listen to this student's response.

Listen to the recording

Aiming higher

Include the following in your speaking and writing, to aim for a higher grade.

- ✓ **Adjectives** make your speaking and writing much more ... fascinating, exciting, amusing.

- ✓ Think PPF (past, present, future) **tenses** before you say anything and then figure out a way to incorporate all three into your answer.

- ✓ **Conjunctions** give lots of scope for great sentences, so make sure you are confident with weil, wenn and dass, and can also have a go with obwohl, bevor and wo.

- ✓ Be prepared for prompts from your teacher such as noch etwas? (anything else?) or warum (nicht)? (why (not)?) to encourage you to add extra detail.

Now try this

Now prepare to answer these questions as fully as you can:
- Übernachtest du gern weg von zu Hause? Warum (nicht)?
- Was war deine beste Übernachtung?
- Wo würdest du gern in Zukunft übernachten?

Try to speak for at least 30 seconds on each point.

Think:
- connectives
- adjectives
- tenses
- conjunctions

Throw each of these into the mix and you are well on the way to a very good answer.

Holiday destinations

Always check your translation carefully – does your English flow well and does your text really make sense?

Ferienziele

Am liebsten übernachte ich ...	I like staying most of all ...
auf dem Land	in the countryside
an der Küste	on the coast
in den Bergen	in the mountains
in einer Stadt	in a town
in einem Dorf	in a village
zu Hause	at home
bei Freunden	with friends

weil man im See schwimmen kann
because you can swim in the lake

weil es dort viel wärmer als in England ist
because it is much warmer there than in England

weil meine Eltern gern in den Bergen wandern gehen
because my parents like walking in the mountains

Dative and accusative prepositions

Grammar page 87

an	on, to, at
auf	on, to
in	in, into

These use the **dative** case when there is **no movement** involved.

Ich wohne im Ausland. I live abroad.
Das Haus liegt am See.
The house is on the lake.

But if there is **movement towards** something, this signals the **accusative** case.

Ich fahre ins Ausland.
I am going abroad.
Ich fahre an die Küste.
I am going to the coast.

Am liebsten übernachte ich an der Küste.

Worked example

READING

Translation
Translate this passage **into English**.　(1 mark)

> Am liebsten übernachte ich am Meer, vor allem wenn das Wetter dort schön ist.

Most of all I like to stay at the seaside, especially when the weather is lovely there.

If you can't remember what **Meer** means, carry on reading for further clues. It is somewhere this person likes to go when the weather is good. Where might it be?

There is often more than one word you can use to translate a word – here, **schön** can be translated as 'lovely', 'fine' or even 'very good'.

Now try this

READING

Now complete the translation.

> Als Familie fahren wir jedes Jahr nach Teneriffa, wo wir immer unseren ersten Tag im größten Wasserpark Europas verbringen. Ich würde auch einen Tagesausflug zur Hauptstadt empfehlen, um die wunderbaren Märkte zu besuchen und viele preiswerte Andenken zu kaufen. Wir fahren seit vier Jahren dorthin und bevor wir hierher gekommen sind, hatten wir immer den Sommerurlaub an der windigen Nordsee gemacht.

(6 marks)

Holiday experiences

Make sure you can use the perfect tense when talking about holidays in the past.

Vergangene Ferien

letzten Sommer	last summer
in den Winterferien	in the winter holidays
letztes Jahr	last year
vor zwei Jahren	two years ago
Ich habe eine Tour gemacht.	I went on a tour.
Er ist nach Rom geflogen.	He flew to Rome.
Wir haben gefaulenzt.	We lazed.

Ich bin Ski gefahren.
I went skiing.

Er ist Bergsteigen gegangen.
He went mountain climbing.

Sie ist schwimmen gegangen.
She went swimming.

Ich bin zelten gegangen.
I went camping.

The perfect tense

Grammar page 100

If you did something in the past, use the perfect tense!

ich habe	
du hast	gekauft (bought)
er / sie / man hat **+**	gemacht (did)
ihr habt	besucht (visited)
wir / Sie / sie haben	gesehen (saw)
ich bin	
du bist	gegangen (went)
er / sie / man ist **+**	geflogen (flew)
ihr seid	gefahren (went / drove)
wir / Sie / sie sind	

To give your opinion in the past, use Es war + adjective:

Es war ...

spektakulär / schön   stinklangweilig / furchtbar

Ich bin nach Berlin gefahren. Es war prima!
I went to Berlin. It was great!

Worked example

LISTENING TRACK 20

Urlaubserlebnisse

Du hörst einen Bericht im Internet über Katjas Urlaub letztes Jahr. Wie war es? Trage entweder **fantastisch**, **enttäuschend**, **langweilig** oder **interessant** ein.

Listen to the recording

Beispiel: Die Übernachtung war .....enttäuschend....

> Letzten Sommer bin ich in den Schwarzwald gefahren. Der Campingplatz sah in der Broschüre wunderbar aus, aber er war in Wirklichkeit dreckig und sehr laut.

Be prepared

- ✓ **Read the rubric** first: this is about 'last year', so you are going to hear past tense sentences.
- ✓ **Look at the four adjectives** to choose from and think about what words you might expect to hear for each one.
- ✓ Remember – you will hear the extract **twice**, so don't panic if you don't get the answer first time round.

Now try this

LISTENING TRACK 21

Now complete the listening activity by selecting the correct adjective for each of these **three** reports. Some words can occur more than once.   **(3 marks)**

Listen to the recording

(a) ....   (b) ....   (c) ....

Holiday activities

For more things you might do on holiday, look at the leisure activities on page 19.

Urlaubsaktivitäten

Man kann …

bergsteigen gehen

segeln

eislaufen gehen

Ski fahren

faulenzen

spazieren gehen

Rad fahren

Tennis spielen

schwimmen gehen

Saying what you can do

The verbs on the left are in the infinitive form – you need to use this form after the expression Man kann … (You can …).

Man kann …	ins Schwimmbad gehen.
You can …	go to the pool.
	sich sonnen. sunbathe.

If you start your sentence with a time or place expression, kann and man swap places.

In den Alpen kann man …
In the Alps you can …

In den Ferien kann man reiten.
In the holidays you can go horse riding.

> Im Schwarzwald kann man auch reiten.

Dealing with unknown words

☑ Break words down to decode them.
– schwarz (black) + Wald (wood) = Black Forest
– frei (free) + Zeit (time) + Park (park) = leisure / theme park
– Bogen (bow) + schießen (shoot) = archery
– wild (wild) + Wasser (water) + rutschen (slide) = white-water slides / flumes

☑ Use any other clues in the text. For example, Bogenschießen is listed as a sport and Wildwasserrutschen can be found in a theme park.

Worked example

READING

Holidays
Read the advert for holiday activities.

> **Verbringen Sie bei uns mitten im Schwarzwald entspannende Tage!**
>
> Hier kann man:
> - viele Sportarten ausprobieren (Bogenschießen, Klettern, Wasserski)
> - herrliche Spaziergänge im Wald machen
> - Tagesausflüge nach Freiburg machen
> - den Freizeitpark mit Wildwasserrutschen besuchen.
>
> „Letzten Sommer haben wir zum ersten Mal eine Woche im Urlaubszentrum verbracht. Wir werden sicher wieder zurückkommen!"

Answer the following qustion **in English**.

(a) Where is the place advertised?   **(1 mark)**

Black Forest

 You won't get a mark if you write **Schwarzwald** – German place names need translating if they are different in English.

Now try this

READING

Now answer these questions on the advert on the left **in English**. You do not need to write in full sentences.

(b) Name **one** sport you can try at the centre.   **(1 mark)**

(c) What can you do in the woods?   **(1 mark)**

(d) What is offered to Freiburg?   **(1 mark)**

(e) What tells you the visitor had a successful time at the centre? **(1 mark)**

Holiday plans

Talking about plans in any topic **will** require the use of the future tense.

Ferienpläne

Ich werde …	I will …
In den Ferien wird er …	In the holidays he will …
Hoffentlich werden sie …	Hopefully they will …
Eines Tages werden wir …	One day we will …
nach Australien fahren.	go to Australia.
zu einem Musikfest gehen.	go to a music festival.
meine Cousine besuchen.	visit my (female) cousin.
nächsten Sommer	next summer
nächsten Winter	next winter
nächstes Jahr	next year
in Zukunft	in future
in zwei Jahren	in two years
Ich freue mich (sehr) darauf.	I am (really) looking forward to it.
Wenn ich älter bin, werde ich einen Ferienjob machen.	When I am older, I will get a holiday job.

Future tense

Grammar page 103

The future tense is formed using a part of werden (to become) + infinitive.

ich	werde
du	wirst
er / sie / man	wird
ihr	werdet
wir / Sie / sie	werden

Ich werde nach Ungarn fahren.
I will go to Hungary.

Sie wird Wasserski fahren.
She will go waterskiing.

If you start your sentence with a time expression, werde and ich swap places.

Nächstes Jahr werde ich zu Hause bleiben.
Next year I will stay at home.

You can also use **hoffen + zu** (to hope to) and **möchten** (would like) to indicate future plans.

Ich hoffe, nächstes Jahr nach Amerika zu fahren.
Next year I hope to go to America.

Worked example

Urlaub
Übersetze **ins Deutsche**.

> Next year I will fly to Germany to visit my girlfriend in Munich.

Nächstes Jahr werde ich nach Deutschland fliegen, um meine Freundin in München zu besuchen.

Aiming higher

✓ Tense markers such as 'next year', 'next week' and 'in future' all scream **future**. Don't translate these using any other tense.

✓ Genders – 'girlfriend' is a feminine noun, so make sure the article or adjective with it is also feminine.

✓ Translate **accurately** – the verb here is 'fly' – don't use fahren!

✓ Munich is an English translation – make sure you use the German name.

Now try this

Now complete the translation **into German**.

> When I was there last time, I got to know some really nice people. We will meet again in May, and will all go on a day trip to the lake. I would rather have a holiday with friends than my family, because that suits me better.

Holiday problems

Watch out for verbs in the present tense that change their vowels!

Urlaubsprobleme

Ich habe ...	I have ...
meinen Reisepass verloren.	lost my passport.
einen Unfall gehabt.	had an accident.
Jemand hat meine Brieftasche genommen / gestohlen.	Somebody has taken / stolen my wallet.
Das Hotelzimmer ...	The hotel room ...
ist schmutzig / laut.	is dirty / loud.
hat keinen Anschluss zum Internet.	has no internet connection.
Der Fernseher ist kaputt.	The television is broken.
Der Kühlschrank funktioniert nicht.	The fridge does not work.
Es sind Haare im Waschbecken.	There is hair in the basin.
Es gibt keine Seife.	There is no soap.

Present tense irregular verbs

geben	nehmen
– to give	– to take
ich gebe	ich nehme
du gibst	du nimmst
er / sie / es gibt	er / sie / es nimmt
ihr gebt	ihr nehmt
wir / Sie / sie geben	wir / Sie / sie nehmen

Negative words

Signs with these words on are warnings **not** to do something!

 nicht
not

 kein
not a / no

 verboten
forbidden

 Achtung
Attention!

Bitte hier nicht rauchen

Schwimmen verboten

Worked example

 SPEAKING

Instructions to candidate:
You are staying in a hotel in Switzerland. You are at the reception desk to report a problem. Your teacher will play the part of the hotel manager and will speak first.

Task
An der Hotelrezeption. Du beschwerst dich über ein Problem.

1 Problem (zwei Details)
– Guten Tag. Wie kann ich Ihnen helfen?
– Der Fernseher im Zimmer funktioniert nicht.

2 Zimmer – Nummer und Stock
– Das tut mir leid. Was ist Ihre Zimmernummer?
– Nummer dreihundertacht im dritten Stock.

3 !
– Woher kommen Sie?
– Aus England.

If you don't catch this unexpected question first time, just ask politely: Wie bitte?

This tells you the content of the conversation: here you are reporting a **problem**, so think of **one** problem you might report at a hotel reception desk. It can be anything – within reason!

This student keeps things simple – and completes the task by giving **two** details about a problem.

Again, this student completes the mission: a room number and floor details.

Now try this

 SPEAKING TRACK 22

Now practise the whole role play yourself, including the final two prompts. Listen to the audio file containing the teacher's part and fill in the pauses with your answers:
4 Urlaubsaktivitäten (zwei Details)
5 ? Abendprogramm

Listen to the recording

Asking for help

Being able to ask for help when you have a problem and suggesting a Lösung (solution) might come up in your Speaking exam as well as being a useful life skill!

Hilfe!

Ich habe eine Panne.
I have broken down.

Haben Sie den Ersatzteil?
Have you got the replacement part?

Wo finde ich das Kundendienst?
Where do I find customer services?

Könnten Sie die Rechnung nachprüfen?
Could you check the bill?

Wo kann ich das Auto reparieren lassen?
Where can I get the car fixed?

Ich habe schreckliche Magenschmerzen.
I have a dreadful stomach ache.

Gibt es hier in der Nähe eine Apotheke?
Is there a pharmacy nearby?

Wo ist die Polizeiwache?
Where is the police station?

Ist diese Urlaubsversicherung noch gültig?
Is this holiday insurance still valid?

Könnten Sie bitte einen Krankenwagen rufen?
Could you please ring for an ambulance?

Saying something hurts

Mein(e) ... tut weh. My ... hurts.
Use tut (one thing) or tun (more than one thing) + weh.

⬇

Mein Fuß tut weh. My foot hurts.

⬇

Meine Füße tun weh. My feet hurt.

You can also talk about past pain:
Meine Hand tat weh. My hand hurt.

⬇

Meine Arme taten weh. My arms hurt.

| Bein (n) | leg | Knie (n) | knee |
| Finger (m) | finger | Schulter (f) | shoulder |

Naming a body part and adding -schmerzen (pain) is an easy way to express what part of your body needs help! Ich habe Kopfschmerzen (I have a headache).

Worked example
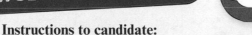

Instructions to candidate:
You have an accident on a skiing holiday in Austria. Your teacher will play the part of a ski instructor and will speak first.

Task
Du bist beim Skiurlaub in Österreich. Du hast einen Unfall auf der Piste und sprichst mit dem Skilehrer / der Skilehrerin.

1 Problem (zwei Details)
– Kann ich Ihnen helfen?
– Mein linkes Bein tut schrecklich weh.

2 Wo – Familie
– Oje! Wo kann ich Ihre Eltern finden?
– Sie sind unten im Dorf in einem großen Hotel.

3 !
– Was ist passiert?
– Ich bin auf der Piste gefallen.

This unexpected question is in the past tense, and the student replies in the past tense too.

Exam alert

Don't be over-ambitious in your role play. Communication is the key, so concentrate on getting the message across from your task sheet.

The two details given here are 'leg' and 'hurts'. Message communicated, along with a nice addition of the adjective 'left'.

Now try this

Now practise the whole role play yourself, including the final two prompts:
4 ? Hilfe – wann
5 ? Holen – was

Listen to the recording

Transport

Don't forget the **time – manner – place** rule when you are writing and translating in German.

Verkehrsmittel

mit dem Auto / Wagen

mit der Bahn / mit dem Zug

mit dem Boot / Schiff

mit dem Bus

mit dem Rad (Fahrrad)

mit dem Flugzeug

mit dem Lastwagen

mit dem Mofa

mit dem Motorrad

mit der Straßenbahn

zu Fuß

DB = Deutsche Bahn
ICE = Inter City-Express

Time – Manner – Place

> Grammar page 92

A detail of transport counts as Manner, so put it **after** a Time expression, but **before** a Place.

 T gestern / heute / letzte Woche / in Zukunft

M mit dem Zug / zu Fuß / mit meiner Familie

P nach London / in die Stadt / über die Brücke

Heute fahre ich mit der U-Bahn in die Stadtmitte. Ich bin letzte Woche mit der Straßenbahn gefahren.

Worked example

WRITING

Die Verkehrsmittel in deiner Stadt
Deine Austauschpartnerin schickt dir Fragen über die Verkehrsmittel in deiner Stadt. Schreibe eine Antwort.

Du **musst** diesen Punkt einschließen:

• wie du in die Stadt fährst.

> Wenn ich samstags mit meinen Freunden in die Stadt fahre, nehmen wir immer die U-Bahn.
> Ich finde, dass die U-Bahn praktisch ist.

Aiming higher

> Ich muss nie länger als fünf Minuten warten jeder Zug kommt pünktlich an.

Great use of singular **ich fahre** and plural **wir nehmen** structures.

Giving an opinion with **Ich denke / finde, dass …** raises the level of your writing.

This student has added a modal verb and used a comparative adjective, which raises the level more.

Now try this

WRITING

Now include the following points and complete the above writing activity:
• wie du zur Schule fährst und warum
• wie du letztes Jahr in den Urlaub gefahren bist und warum
• ob du als Erwachsene/r lieber mit dem Auto oder mit dem Bus fahren wirst und warum.

Schreibe ungefähr 80–90 Wörter **auf Deutsch**.

Travel

Whether it is by car, train or plane, travelling is part of life, so make sure you are secure with the vocabulary on this page.

Unterwegs

Autobahn (f)	motorway
Benzin (n)	petrol
Fahrt (f)	journey
Hubschrauber (m)	helicopter
Motor (m)	engine
Passagier (m)	passenger
Raststätte (f)	motorway services
Stau (m)	traffic jam
Stoßzeit (f)	rush hour
Tankstelle (f)	petrol station
Umleitung (f)	diversion
öffentliche Verkehrsmittel (npl)	public transport
Verspätung haben	to be delayed

Opinions

Use Ich glaube, dass (I believe that) or Ich finde, dass (I think that) as handy ways to add an opinion. Dass sends the verb to the end of the clause.

Fahrradwege sind ausgezeichnet.
Cycle paths are excellent.

⬇

Ich finde, dass Fahrradwege ausgezeichnet sind.
I think that cycle paths are excellent.

Here are some other adjectives you could use when talking about transport:

bequem	comfortable
praktisch	practical
pünktlich	punctual
schädlich	harmful
umweltfreundlich	environmentally friendly

 Worked example

Travelling
Read the opinions about travelling.

> **Barbara:** Meiner Meinung nach sollte jeder versuchen, öfter mit der Bahn oder mit dem Rad zu fahren, weil die immer steigenden Benzinpreise und die Umweltverschmutzung das Autofahren immer unakzeptabler machen.
>
> **Jake:** Ich finde, es ist erstaunlich, wie viel besser die öffentlichen Verkehrsmittel hier in Berlin sind als bei mir zu Hause in England. Wenn man bei uns mehr Geld in Züge investieren würde, könnten wir vielleicht auch stolz auf unser Verkehrsnetz sein!

Answer the following **in English**.

(a) Give **two** reasons why Barbara thinks people should travel by train or bike more. **(2 marks)**

Rising petrol prices and environmental pollution are both reasons why people should use trains or bikes more.

The first part of the sentence tells you that Barbara thinks people should travel by train or bike more – so it is the next part which will provide your answer.

 erstaunlich – incredible
stolz auf – proud of

Exam alert

When you are asked a question in English you have to **answer** in English. You will not score if you answer in German. Also, if the question asks for **two** reasons, make sure you don't write one or three. If you write three, the third one will be ignored.

Now try this

Now answer these questions on Jake's opinion. You do not need to answer in full sentences.
(b) What does Jake think of the public transport in Berlin? **(1 mark)**
(c) What would make transport better in England? **(1 mark)**

Directions

Practise your directions in German by giving yourself a running commentary in your head while you are out and about!

Richtungen

Gehen Sie ...   Go ... (on foot)
Fahren Sie ...   Drive

geradeaus   straight on

links um die Ecke
left at the corner

← links   left   → rechts   right

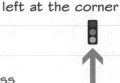
über die Brücke
over the bridge

über den Fluss
over the river

zur Ampel
to the traffic lights

an der Kreuzung links
left at the crossroads

zum Kreisverkehr
to the roundabout

auf der linken Seite
on the left

Instructions using Sie

Grammar page 97

Use the Sie form (-en) of the verb + Sie:
Überqueren Sie die Straße.   Cross the road.
Gehen Sie an der Ampel rechts.
Go right at the lights.

Instructions using du

Use the du form minus the final -st:
Geh die Einbahnstraße hinunter.
Go down the one-way street.

Learning vocabulary

✓ Make your own learning cards – German on one side, English on the other; or a picture on one side, German on the other.

✓ Use learning cards to help you revise. Write key words on them as well as structures you find tricky.

an der Kreuzung links

Worked example

LISTENING TRACK 24

Listen to the recording

Giving directions
You hear people being given directions.

Listen to the recording and put a cross ✗ in the correct box.

Example: To get to the marketplace, go ...

☐ **A** right first of all
☒ **B** over the footbridge
☐ **C** past the lights
☐ **D** left after 100 metres

— Zum Marktplatz gehen Sie hier gleich links und dann 100 Meter geradeaus. Sie kommen dann zum Fluss, wo es eine Fußgängerbrücke gibt. Gehen Sie hinüber und Sie sehen den Marktplatz auf der rechten Seite.

Exam alert

In multiple-choice questions, prepare yourself before you listen by trying to say the options to yourself in German. You will be better prepared when you listen!

Now try this

LISTENING TRACK 25

Listen to the recording

Now complete the listening activity by selecting the correct option from the worked example for each of these **three** further directions.   **(3 marks)**

(a) ☐   (b) ☐   (c) ☐

Eating in a café

Lots of these food words look very similar to English, so you should recognise them in a reading or listening passage.

Im Café essen

Bratwurst (f)	fried sausage
Erfrischungen (pl)	refreshments
Frikadelle (f)	meatball
Fruchtsaft (m)	fruit juice
Hamburger (m)	hamburger
heiße Schokolade (f)	hot chocolate
Imbiss (m)	snack
Mineralwasser (n)	mineral water
Omelett (n)	omelette
Pommes (frites) (pl)	chips
Salat (m)	salad
Schinkenbrot (n)	ham sandwich
Schnellimbiss (m)	snack bar
Selbstbedienung (f)	self-service
Spiegelei (n)	fried egg
Einmal / Zweimal … bitte.	One / Two portion(s) of … please.

Indefinite article (a, an)

Grammar page 86

Masculine nouns

- nominative – ein
  Ein Kaffee kostet 3 Euro.
  A coffee costs 3 euros.

- accusative – einen
  Ich hätte gern einen Kaffee.
  I'd like a coffee.

Feminine nouns

- nominative and accusative – eine
  Eine Limonade kostet 2,50 Euro.
  A lemonade costs 2.50 euros.
  Ich hätte gern eine Limonade.
  I'd like a lemonade.

Neuter nouns

- nominative and accusative – ein
  Ein Käsebrot kostet 4 Euro.
  A cheese sandwich costs 4 euros.
  Ich hätte gern ein Käsebrötchen.
  I'd like a cheese roll.

There is no need for 'of' in German when talking about quantities!
eine Tasse Tee – a cup of tea
ein Stück Torte – a piece of gateau

Worked example

Translation
Translate this passage **into English**.   **(3 marks)**

> Samstags gehe ich oft mit meiner Mutter ins Café. Ich bestelle gern eine Limonade und eine Portion Pommes.

Don't miss out **gern** here – what does it tell you?

On Saturdays I often go with my mum to the café. I like to order a lemonade and a portion of chips.

Identifying tenses

✓ Use **key words** to help identify the tense of each sentence in a translation:

– jetzt (now) and im Moment (at the moment) tell you something is happening now, i.e. in the present tense

– früher (earlier) and gestern (yesterday) indicate the past tense

– nächste Woche (next week) is a future tense time marker.

✓ Use **grammar** to help identify tenses:

– verbs ending in -e, -t, -st, etc. indicate the present tense: ich gehe, sie schläft

– part of haben or sein and a participle starting with ge- at the end of a clause indicates the past tense

– part of werden plus an infinitive at the end indicates the future tense.

Now try this

Now complete the translation.

> Das letzte Mal hat meine Mutter ein Spiegelei bestellt. Nächstes Mal wird sie das nicht wieder bestellen.

(4 marks)

Don't miss out **wieder** here – what does it tell you?

Eating in a restaurant

A restaurant setting might be the focus for an activity, so prepare with this page.

Im Restaurant

Speisekarte (f)	menu
Speisesaal (m)	dining room
Tagesgericht (n)	dish of the day
Menü (n)	set meal
Getränk (n)	drink
Vorspeise (f)	starter
Hauptgericht (n)	main course
Nachspeise (f)	dessert
Gabel (f)	fork
Geschirr (n)	crockery
Löffel (m)	spoon
Messer (n)	knife
Teller (m)	plate
gebraten	roast
gekocht	cooked

Using wenn

Grammar page 93

Try to include a complex sentence using wenn to improve your work.

Wenn ich Hunger hätte, würde ich Frikadellen mit Pommes bestellen.

If I were hungry, I would order meatballs and chips.

Wenn ich Vegetarier wäre, würde ich meistens italienisch essen.

If I were a vegetarian, I would eat mostly Italian food.

Listening strategies

- ✓ Cognates are easy to spot when you see them, but they can sound slightly different – here Blog sounds more like 'block', so ask yourself which is more likely in this context?
- ✓ Listening extracts will have a selection of vocabulary from across all the topics – just because this is titled 'Restaurants in Germany', it does not mean that what you hear will be exclusively restaurant-themed vocabulary.

Worked example

  LISTENING TRACK 26

Restaurants in Germany
You hear an interview about local restaurants.

Listen to the recording and complete the sentence by putting a cross ✗ in the correct box.

Example: This diner chose the restaurant because …

☐ **A** of the menu.

☐ **B** of the location.

☒ **C** of a recommendation.

☐ **D** it is new

 Listen to the recording

— Welches Restaurant hast du besucht?

— Das neue gegenüber dem Dom. Das ist eine gute Strecke weg, aber ein Freund hatte es auf seinem Blog beschrieben, also wollte ich es selbst ausprobieren. Er war sehr begeistert davon, aber ich habe die Speisen ziemlich enttäuschend gefunden, muss ich sagen.

Now try this

 LISTENING TRACK 27

Now complete the listening activity by selecting the correct option for these **three** recordings.   **(3 marks)**

This diner chose the restaurant because …

(a) ☐ **A** of the view.

☐ **B** of the location.

☐ **C** of the prices.

☐ **D** of the chef.

(b) ☐ **A** it is cheap.

☐ **B** it is easy to get to.

☐ **C** it was good last time.

☐ **D** it is new.

(c) ☐ **A** of the menu.

☐ **B** friends own it.

☐ **C** of a recommendation.

☐ **D** it is fashionable.

 Listen to the recording

This speaker says the restaurant is **neu** (option D), but that is not **why** she chose it.

Shopping for food

To buy fruit and vegetables, add a quantity first: ein Kilo (Äpfel) or 400 Gramm (Pilze), bitte! Note that there is no word for 'of' in this context in German.

Auf dem Markt

Obst	Fruit	Gemüse	Vegetables
Ananas (f)	pineapple	Blumenkohl(-e) (m)	cauliflower
Apfel(¨) (m)	apple	Bohne(-n) (f)	bean
Apfelsine(-n) (f) / Orange(-n) (f)	orange	Erbse(-n) (f)	pea
		Gurke(-n) (f)	cucumber
Aprikose(-n) (f)	apricot	Karotte(-n) (f)	carrot
Banane(-n) (f)	banana	Kartoffel(-n) (f)	potato
Birne(-n) (f)	pear	Knoblauch (m)	garlic
Erdbeere(-n) (f)	strawberry	Kohl(-e) (m)	cabbage
Himbeere(-n) (f)	raspberry	Kopfsalat(-e) (m)	lettuce
Kirsche(-n) (f)	cherry	Pilz(-e) (m)	mushroom
Pfirsich(-e) (m)	peach	Rosenkohl (m)	Brussels sprout
Pflaume(-n) (f)	plum	Spinat (m)	spinach
Tomate(-n) (f)	tomato	Zwiebel(-n) (f)	onion
Traube(-n) (f)	grape		

Plurals

German nouns all have different plurals. You can look in a dictionary if you are unsure.

An online search for 'Kartoffel plural' gives you the answer instantly:

> Kartoffel (f) (genitive der Kartoffel, plural die Kartoffeln) – potato

The nominative plural word for 'the' is always **die**.

Reading tips

☑ Go through the text and underline the nouns that are fruit and vegetables – they start with a **capital letter**.

☑ Use cognates, such as: Karotten (carrots), and words with a link to an English word: Gurken (cucumbers), from 'gherkin'.

Worked example

Shopping for food
Read what these people are buying.

> **Alex** Ich kaufe immer Karotten und manchmal kaufe ich auch eine Gurke.
> **Kai** Im Sommer kaufe ich gern Erdbeeren und Himbeeren, aber im Winter kaufe ich kein Obst.
> **Petra** Ich kaufe oft online, und ich klicke immer Erbsen und Bohnen an, denn sie sind lecker.
> **Edi** Ich kaufe jede Woche ein Kilo Kartoffeln, denn ich liebe Pommes. Ich kaufe auch immer Kirschen, denn das ist mein Lieblingsobst.

Who says what about fruit and vegetables?
Answer either **Alex**, **Kai**, **Petra** or **Edi**.

Example: .Edi. buys potatoes.

Exam alert

Just because one person has already been the answer to a question, it does not mean they can't still be the answer to another question. Always read the rubric carefully.

Now try this

Now complete the reading activity. You can use each person more than once.
(a) .... finds peas tasty. **(1 mark)**
(b) .... sometimes buys a cucumber. **(1 mark)**
(c) .... doesn't always buy fruit. **(1 mark)**
(d) .... loves chips. **(1 mark)**
(e) .... buys vegetables on the computer. **(1 mark)**

Opinions about food

If you are giving an opinion on food (or anything else), always justify it: 'I would recommend the restaurant **because** the staff are so friendly.'

Meinungen über das Essen

mein Lieblingsessen	my favourite food
lecker / schmackhaft	tasty
(un)gesund	(un)healthy
ekelhaft / eklig	disgusting
salzig	salty

Es hat mir (nicht) geschmeckt.
I liked (didn't like) it.

Ich würde das Restaurant (nicht) empfehlen.
I would (not) recommend the restaurant.

Es gab eine große / kleine Auswahl an Gerichten.
There was a big / small selection of dishes.

Meiner Meinung nach war es teuer / billig.
In my opinion it was expensive / cheap.

Ich fand die Vorspeise zu scharf.
I found the starter too spicy.

Das Hähnchen hat besonders gut geschmeckt.
The chicken was particularly tasty.

Ich kann Fastfood nicht ausstehen / leiden.
I can't stand fast food.

Imperfect tense

Es ist teuer.	It is expensive.
Es war teuer.	It was expensive.
Ich habe Hunger.	I'm hungry.
Ich hatte Hunger.	I was hungry.
Es gibt kein Besteck.	There's no cutlery.
Es gab kein Besteck.	There wasn't any cutlery.

Note the **plural** forms:

Die Tischtücher waren schmutzig.
The tablecloths were dirty.

Meine Freunde hatten Hunger.
My friends were hungry.

Es gab viele Gläser.
There were a lot of glasses.

Worked example

 LISTENING TRACK 28

Restaurants
You hear an interview on local radio about a restaurant visit.

Listen to the interview and answer the following question in English.

Listen to the recording

(a) Why was Stefan's sister disappointed? **(1 mark)**

soup was very salty

> – Hat das Essen geschmeckt?
>
> – Mir ja, aber meine Schwester fand die Suppe sehr salzig.

Exam alert

You must be precise in your answers to gain the marks. Here, it is specifically the **soup** that was **very salty** so that needs to be written down. You must avoid giving vague answers.

If you don't understand **unhöflich** (rude), it is still worth thinking of an answer after the second hearing rather than leaving a blank. The speaker's **tone of voice** indicates it is something negative, so guess a negative characteristic that a waiter might have.

Now try this

 LISTENING TRACK 29

Now listen to the rest of the interview and answer the following questions **in English**.

Listen to the recording

(b) How did Stefan describe the waiter? **(1 mark)**
(c) Why would Stefan recommend the restaurant to friends? Give **two** reasons. **(2 marks)**

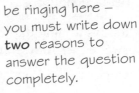

Alarm bells should be ringing here – you must write down **two** reasons to answer the question completely.

Buying gifts

Make sure you are familiar with German numbers (see page 108) so you can deal with euro prices on purchases.

Geschenke kaufen

Abteilung (f)	department
Andenken (n)	souvenir
Auswahl / Wahl (f)	choice
Bedienung (f)	service
Einkaufszentrum (n)	shopping centre
Ermäßigung (f)	reduction
Laden (m) / Geschäft (n)	shop
Notausgang (m)	emergency exit
Quittung (f)	receipt
Schaufenster (n)	shop window
kaufen	to buy
verkaufen	to sell
billig	cheap
preiswert	good value for money
an der Kasse zahlen	to pay at the till

Money

100 Cents = 1 Euro

 ein 10-Euro-Schein

 ein 2-Euro-Stück

Be careful with -zehn and -zig numbers in prices.

fünfzehn = 15   fünfzig = 50

siebzehn = 17   siebzig = 70

If you are noting down a price you hear, make sure you get the numbers the right way round:

vierunddreißig = 4 + 30 = 34

Worked example

READING

Emil und die Detektive **by Erich Kästner**
Read the extract from the text.

Emil has arrived in Berlin from his village to visit his grandmother.

> So ein Krach! Und die vielen Menschen auf den Fußsteigen! Und von allen Seiten Straßenbahnen, Fuhrwerke, zweistöckige Autobusse! Zeitungsverkäufer an allen Ecken.
>
> Wunderbare Schaufenster mit Blumen, Früchten, Büchern, goldenen Uhren, Kleidern und seidener Wäsche. Und hohe, hohe Häuser.
>
> Das war alles Berlin.

Answer the following question **in English**.

(a) What is Emil's first impression of Berlin?   **(1 mark)**

noisy

Dealing with a literary text

- ✓ Don't be afraid of literary texts. They are no different from any other text in the Reading exam – and they give you an interesting insight into German culture.
- ✓ Use the same strategies as you would with any extract – cognates, context and reading the questions to see which words you really do need to focus on.
- ✓ The answers in English have to be precise, but there is often more than one way of relaying each answer. For example, the answer to the example question could be 'busy' or 'hectic', as well as 'noisy'.
- ✓ You will need to use your own words to answer these questions – read the extract through to get the gist first, so you can create a picture of the action in your head.

Now try this

READING

Now answer these **three** further questions on the extract **in English**. You do not need to write in full sentences.

(b) What is Emil's impression of the shops?   **(1 mark)**

(c) Why do you think the shops might have looked expensive to Emil?   **(1 mark)**

(d) What strikes Emil about Berlin, apart from the shops and the transport?   **(1 mark)**

Weather

There are lots of cognates in weather vocabulary, so it shouldn't take you long to master these.

Das Wetter

 Es ist sonnig.   Es ist kalt.   Es ist neblig.

 Es ist windig.   Es ist heiß.   Es schneit.

 Es ist bewölkt / wolkig.   Es regnet.   Es donnert und blitzt.

Es friert.   It's freezing.
Es hagelt.   It's hailing.
Jahreszeit (f) season
im Frühling   in spring   im Herbst   in autumn
im Sommer   in summer   im Winter   in winter

Weather in different tenses

Add value to these weather expressions by adapting them to different tenses.

Present: Es regnet. It is raining.
Imperfect: Es war regnerisch / Es regnete. It was rainy / raining.
Perfect: Es hat geregnet. It rained.
Pluperfect: Es hatte geregnet. It had rained.
Future: Es wird regnen. It will rain.

More weather words in different tenses:

Es ist / war …		It is / was …	
Es wird … sein.		It will be …	
bedeckt	overcast	nass	wet
frostig	frosty	schlecht	bad
heiter	bright	trocken	dry

Exam alert

Look out for the **detail**: 'strong winds' is option **D**, but weaker winds are the only type mentioned in the text, so **D** can't be right.

Worked example

Weather
Read the weather forecast.

Nach Osten hin wird der Wind am Dienstag immer schwächer werden. Höchstwerte liegen bei −14 Grad am Alpenrand und bis −1 Grad an der Ostseeküste. Die Nacht über wird es stark schneien. Es bleibt weiterhin bedeckt.

Put a cross ✗ in the correct box.

Example: What sort of weather is heading for this area?

☐ **A** sunshine
☐ **B** hail
☒ **C** snow
☐ **D** strong winds

- Read to the very end of the report to find the word **bedeckt** (cloudy), so you can rule out **A** 'sunshine'.
- Can you find any reference to hail or hailing in the report? If not, the answer can't be **B** either.
- The minus temperatures and the verb **schneien** (to snow) in the future tense tell you that snow is on the way – answer **C**.

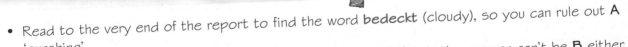

Now try this

Read the report again and put a cross ✗ in the correct box for these two further questions.

(a) What is the wind report?
☐ **A** It will be stronger
☐ **B** It is weaker than on Tuesday
☐ **C** It is blowing from the north
☐ **D** It will be weaker   **(1 mark)**

(b) What is the report for the Alps?
☐ **A** It will be colder than the coast
☐ **B** It will be as cold as the coast
☐ **C** It will have rain
☐ **D** It will have a mild night   **(1 mark)**

Places to see

When you talk or write about sights you have visited, try to include some comparatives or superlatives to improve your answer.

Sehenswürdigkeiten

Brücke (f)	bridge
Brunnen (m)	fountain
Denkmal (n)	monument
Dom (m)	cathedral
Fluss (m)	river
Hafen (m)	port
Kirche (f)	church
Kunstgalerie (f)	art gallery
Markt(platz) (m)	market (square)
Museum (n)	museum
Palast (m)	palace
Rathaus (n)	town hall
Schloss (n) / Burg (f)	castle
Stadion (n)	stadium
Theater (n)	theatre
Tiergarten (m) / Zoo (m)	zoo
Turm (m)	tower
historisch	historic
malerisch	picturesque
sehenswert	worth seeing

Comparisons

Grammar page 90

Make your writing more interesting by using **comparatives** and **superlatives**.

Meine Stadt ist ... My town is ...	interessant. interesting.
	interessanter als Hamburg. more interesting than Hamburg.
	am interessantesten. the most interesting.
	eine der interessantesten Städte in Deutschland. one of the most interesting towns in Germany.

Florenz ist die schönste Stadt, die ich je besucht habe.

 Worked example READING

Tourism
Read this tourist information. Answer the following question **in English**.

Entdecken Sie Rothenburg – die schönste Stadt Deutschlands

Rothenburg ist eines der beliebtesten Touristenziele in Deutschland. Die kleine Stadt hat viele historische Gebäude wie das Burgtor und das Rathaus, das zu den ältesten Gebäuden der Stadt zählt. Weitere Informationen findet man beim Verkehrsamt in der Innenstadt. Gehen Sie dorthin, um die günstigsten Theaterkarten zu reservieren.

(a) Where can you book theatre tickets? **(1 mark)**

You can book tickets at the tourist office.

Stadtzentrum   hin – to
Stadtzentrum   her – from

 Now try this READING

Now answer these **four** further questions on the text **in English**. You do not need to write in full sentences.

(b) How do you know Rothenburg receives lots of visitors? **(1 mark)**

(c) Why do you think not many people live there? **(1 mark)**

(d) Why might tourists be especially interested in the town hall? **(1 mark)**

(e) Where exactly is the tourist office? **(1 mark)**

At the tourist office

Make sure you are familiar with the places in town vocabulary from page 47 in case you have a role play situation at the tourist office.

Beim Verkehrsamt

Ausflug (m)	trip, outing
Ausstellung (f)	exhibition
Broschüre (f)	brochure
Eintrittsgeld (n)	entry fee
Eintrittskarte (f)	entry ticket
Ermäßigung (f)	reduction
Fahrradverleih (m)	bicycle hire
Hotelverzeichnis (n)	hotel list
Öffnungszeiten (pl)	opening hours
Reservierung (f)	reservation
Rundgang (m)	tour (on foot)
Rundfahrt (f)	tour (by transport)
Veranstaltung (f)	event
geschlossen	closed
geöffnet	open
Guten Aufenthalt!	Enjoy your stay!
im Voraus	in advance

Using weil, dass, wo (because, that, where)

Grammar page 93

Don't be worried by conjunctions that send the verb to the end of the sentence. Learn a few key phrases and it will become natural.

Ich möchte ein Fahrrad mieten, weil die Fahrradwege hier sehr gut sind.
I would like to hire a bike, because the cycle paths are very good here.

Möchten Sie, dass ich die Eintrittskarten reserviere?
Would you like me to reserve the entry tickets for you?

Ist das die Ausstellung, wo es moderne Kunst gibt?
Is that the exhibition where there is modern art?

Wir möchten wissen, wo es hier einen Fahrradverleih gibt.

Worked example

Instructions to candidate:
You are asking for information in the tourist office in Germany. Your teacher will play the role of the tourist information employee and will speak first.

Task
Du suchst Informationen beim Verkehrsamt in einer deutschen Stadt.

1 Meinung über die Stadt und Grund
 – Willkommen! Wie finden Sie unsere Stadt?
– Danke. Die Stadt gefällt mir besonders gut, weil die alten Gebäude so schön sind.

2 Ausflug – Tag und wohin
 – Sehr gut. Wie kann ich Ihnen helfen?
– Ich möchte am Mittwoch an die Küste fahren.

3 !
 – Toll. Hier ist eine Broschüre. Was haben Sie gestern gemacht?
– Ich habe das Stadtmuseum besucht.
 – Sehr schön.

Aiming higher

✓ Don't lose sight of the question you are being asked or the statement you are responding to. First and foremost in the role play, you need to provide the answer to your prompts.

✓ Make sure you pronounce the German words accurately, and aim to use the correct articles and adjective endings, as this will make your work stand out. In a good way!

An opinion and a reason are needed here. Stay focused to ensure you don't miss either of them out! Here, the use of weil + verb to the end shows a competent command of German.

Now try this

Now practise the whole role play yourself, including the final two prompts:
4   ? Etwas kaufen – wo
5   ? Geschäft – Zeiten

Listen to the recording

Describing a town

Learn these words so you can write or speak about towns you have visited.

In der Stadt

Bäckerei (f)	baker's
Bahnhof (m)	station
Bank (f)	bank
Bowling (n)	tenpin bowling
Buchhandlung (f)	bookshop
Eishalle (f)	ice rink
Freizeitpark (m)	theme park
Freizeitzentrum (n)	leisure centre
Hallenbad (n)	indoor swimming pool
Kaufhaus (n)	department store
Kino (n)	cinema
Kneipe (f) / Lokal (n)	pub
Lebensmittelgeschäft (n)	grocer's
Markt (m)	market
Polizeiwache (f)	police station
Tankstelle (f)	service station
Waschsalon (m)	launderette
Zeitungskiosk (m)	newspaper stall

Es gibt ... (there is / are ...)

Use es gibt + accusative (einen, eine, ein) in different tenses to help improve your speaking and writing.

Present: Es gibt ... There is ...

Imperfect: Als ich klein war, gab es ... When I was young, there was ...

Pluperfect: Vorher hatte es ... gegeben. Earlier there had been ...

Future: In Zukunft wird es ... geben. In future there will be ...

Conditional: In meiner idealen Stadt gäbe es ... In my ideal town there would be ...

... eine Eishalle

Adjectives

Make sure you have a good supply of adjectives to express your opinion.

😊				😞		😐	
großartig	magnificent	sauber	clean	dreckig / schmutzig	dirty	flach	flat
hübsch	pretty	malerisch	picturesque	industriell	industrial	ruhig	quiet

Worked example

Freizeit
Übersetze **ins Deutsche**.

There is a leisure centre in my town.　**(2 marks)**

In meiner Stadt gibt es ein Freizeitzentrum.

Translating into German

☑ Read the English sentence carefully and check you understand it properly: who or what is it talking about?

☑ It doesn't matter if you start with In meiner Stadt or Es, but you **must** put the verb gibt next so it is in **second** position.

Now try this

Now translate these sentences **into German**.

(a) The department store is very old and expensive. **(2 marks)**
(b) I prefer to shop at the market. **(2 marks)**
(c) Yesterday I went to the cinema. **(2 marks)**
(d) My brother stayed at home because he was tired. **(2 marks)**

Two ways of saying 'because':
denn – no change to word order
weil – verb to end of clause.
Can't remember 'tired' in German?
How about **hatte keine Energie**?

Describing a region

Make sure you know the points of the compass, so you can be specific when describing where places are located.

Eine Gegend

Autobahn (f)	motorway	Landschaft (f)	landscape
Badeort (m)	seaside resort	Natur (f)	nature
Berg (m)	mountain	Ort (m)	place
Bundesstraße (f)	main road	See (f) / Meer (n)	sea
Bürgersteig (m)	pavement	See (m)	lake
Dorf (n)	village	Stadtrand (m)	outskirts (of town)
Einwohner (m)	inhabitant	Stadtviertel (n) /	area of town
Feld (n)	field	Stadtteil (m)	
Gebiet (n)	area	Strand (m)	beach
Großstadt (f)	big city	Umgebung (f)	surrounding area
Hügel (m)	hill	Vorort (m)	suburb
Insel (f)	island	Wald (m)	forest, wood
Küste (f)	coast	sich befinden	to be situated
Land (n)	(German) state		

North, South, East, West

im Norden

im Westen   im Osten

im Süden

To say NE, NW, SE, SW:
in Südwestengland – in south-west England
in Nordostschottland – in north-east Scotland

Describing a region

- When saying where a region is, offer plenty of information and include adjectives (malerisch, einmalig) and interesting verbs (zählt, liegt, umgeben).
- Here is a top-level piece of writing: Der Schwarzwald ist ein malerisches Gebiet, das sich im Südwesten von Deutschland befindet. Die hübschen Städte in dieser Gegend sind von zahlreichen Wäldern und einer großartigen Landschaft umgeben.

Köln – Cologne
München – Munich
Wien – Vienna
Bayern – Bavaria
der Bodensee – Lake Constance
die Donau – Danube
der Ärmelkanal – the English Channel

Worked example

LISTENING TRACK 31

Travel and tourism
You hear this radio advertisement for the Black Forest.

What do you find out about it?

Look at the example and listen to the recording.

Listen to the recording

Example: ☒ The Black Forest is in south-west Germany.

- ☐ **A** It is an industrial area.
- ☐ **B** You can swim in its lakes.
- ☐ **C** It has good weather.
- ☐ **D** It has lovely mountains.
- ☐ **E** The Danube has its origins here.
- ☐ **F** It is never sunny.
- ☐ **G** Its river is not well known.

— Der Schwarzwald ist ein wunderbares Gebiet in Südwestdeutschland.

Now try this

LISTENING TRACK 32

Now listen to the rest of the recording and put a cross by **three** more correct statements.

(3 marks)

Listen to the recording

Tourism

Look at page 47 for places in your town which might be popular with tourists.

Die Touristik

Alpen (pl)	Alps
Anmeldung (f)	registration, booking in
Aufenthalt (m)	stay
im Ausland	abroad
Ausländer/in (m/f)	foreigner
Besuch (m)	visit
Flughafen (m)	airport
Gastfreundschaft (f)	hospitality
Grünanlage (f) / Park (m)	park
Informationsbüro (n)	information office
Parkplatz (m)	car park
Pauschalreise (f)	package holiday
Postkarte (f)	postcard
Reisebus (m)	coach
Tour (f)	tour
Tourist/in (m/f)	tourist
Verkehr (m)	traffic
Verkehrsamt (n)	tourist office

Definite article (the)

Grammar page 85

Three genders and a plural make up the German words for 'the'.

der – masculine	
die – feminine	die – all plurals
das – neuter	

masculine – Der Besuch war erfolgreich.
The visit was successful.
feminine – Die Grünanlage hat auch einen Spielplatz.
The park also has a playground.
neuter – Das Verkehrsamt ist montags geschlossen.
The tourist office is closed on Mondays.
plural – Die Alpen sind großartig.
The Alps are magnificent.

Picture-based task (Foundation)

In your preparation time:

☑ make sure you can **describe** the picture by recalling plenty of relevant adjectives, such as rot, groß, schön, as well as positional words: in, auf der linken Seite, hier im Zentrum and so on.

☑ consider the **four** points that you will have to speak about. Spend a few minutes on each one, noting the tenses you can use and any useful phrases, but remember: you **must not** read out whole prepared sentences.

Worked example

Tourist activities

Schau dir das Foto an und sei bereit, über Folgendes zu sprechen:
• Beschreibung des Fotos.

Das Foto hat man in den Alpen gemacht, denke ich. Die Landschaft ist schön und ruhig, und hier gibt es viele Touristen draußen vor einem Café. Sie sitzen alle in der Sonne, um zu chillen. Meiner Meinung nach sind sie vorher Ski gefahren, und jetzt wollen sie sich ausruhen. Skifahren muss anstrengend sein!

Now try this

Now prepare to talk on the subject of these bullet points as fully as you can:
• Ob Skifahren umweltfreundlich ist
• Erzählung von einem Besuch in einer touristischen Stadt
• Was du gern im Urlaub machst
• Wo du nächstes Jahr Urlaub machen willst.
Try to speak for at least 30 seconds on each point.

Countries

Learn countries and nationalities together. Many of them sound like English!

Länder			
Country	upper case	lower case	Adjective
Deutschland	der Deutsche / ein Deutscher	die / eine Deutsche	deutsch
England	Engländer	Engländerin	englisch
Frankreich	Franzose	Französin	französisch
Großbritannien	Brite	Britin	britisch
Irland	Ire	Irin	irisch
Italien	Italiener	Italienerin	italienisch
Österreich	Österreicher	Österreicherin	österreichisch
Schottland	Schotte	Schottin	schottisch
Spanien	Spanier	Spanierin	spanisch
Wales	Waliser	Waliserin	walisisch
die Schweiz	Schweizer	Schweizerin	schweizerisch
die Türkei	Türke	Türkin	türkisch
die Vereinigten Staaten	Amerikaner	Amerikanerin	amerikanisch

Worked example

Dein letzter Urlaub

Du nimmst an einem Urlaubswettbewerb teil.

Schreibe einen Artikel über deinen letzten Urlaub.

Du **musst** diesen Punkt einschließen:

• Details über den Urlaub.

Obwohl ich letzten Sommer zwei Wochen Urlaub in Italien gemacht habe, hat es mir nicht besonders gut gefallen, weil das Wetter sehr schlecht war.

This is the first part of this student's answer.

Exam alert

• In the Higher Writing paper you have to choose **one** topic from a choice of **two** to write about. Make sure you spend enough time selecting the topic you will be able to write best about – you will not have time to change your mind halfway through the task.

• Keep a count of the bullet points and your words: here, there are four bullet points, so divide the essay length (130–150 words) by four to remind yourself to write about 35 words for each bullet point.

Aiming higher

For a higher grade, try to include:

✓ a subordinating conjunction, such as obwohl (although)

✓ dative expressions, such as es hat mir gefallen.

Now try this

Now include the following points and complete the writing activity:
• was du gemacht hast
• warum andere Leute diesen Urlaub (nicht) genießen würden
• was du im nächsten Urlaub unternehmen wirst.

Rechtfertige deine Ideen und Meinungen.

Schreibe ungefähr 130–150 Wörter **auf Deutsch**.

School subjects

Knowledge of school subject vocabulary is essential for Listening and Reading exams.

Schulfächer

Mathe　Biologie　Chemie

Physik　Deutsch　Englisch

Französisch　Spanisch　Erdkunde

Geschichte　Religion　Informatik

Kunst　Sport　Turnen

Seit + present tense

To talk about how long you have been doing something, use seit + present tense.

Ich lerne seit vier Jahren Deutsch.
I have been learning German for four years.

Seit (since) is followed by the dative case.

seit vier Monaten — Dative plurals add -n!
for four months
seit diesem Trimester　for this term
seit letztem Jahr　since last year
seit letzter Woche　since last week

Other useful vocabulary:
Pflichtfach (n) — compulsory subject
Theater (n) — drama
Wahlfach (n) — optional subject
Werken (n) — DT

Worked example

Olaf's school day

You hear Olaf talking about his day at school. What do you find out?

(a) Listen to the recording and complete the sentence by putting a cross ✗ in the correct box.

Example: On Tuesday Olaf arrived at school …

☐ **A** by bike
☐ **B** on time
☒ **C** late
☐ **D** early

— Am Dienstag habe ich den Bus verpasst und ich bin leider zu spät in der Schule angekommen.

Exam alert

Knowledge of vocabulary is essential for Listening exams. Olaf says **ich bin leider zu spät in der Schule angekommen**. If you didn't know that **spät** means 'late', did you pick up on the word **leider** to give you a further clue?

spät — late
zu spät — too late
die Verspätung — delay

Now try this

Now listen to the rest of the recording and put a cross ✗ in the correct box for each sentence.

(b) At breaktime Olaf …
☐ **A** had a detention.
☐ **B** had fun.
☐ **C** was with friends.
☐ **D** played.　**(1 mark)**

(c) In the first lesson Olaf …
☐ **A** had his favourite subject.
☐ **B** was in a science room.
☐ **C** got on well with his partner.
☐ **D** annoyed his partner.　**(1 mark)**

Opinions about school

You may be asked to express your opinion about school in at least one part of the Speaking exam – the role play, talking about a photo or in general conversation.

Meinungen über die Schule

Meiner Meinung nach ist Chemie viel einfacher als Biologie.
In my opinion chemistry is much easier than biology.

Ich finde, dass Mathe sehr schwierig ist.
I think that maths is very difficult.

Ich bin stark / schwach in Deutsch.
I am good / weak in German.

Es ist gut, dass ich in der Schule oft erfolgreich bin.
It's good that I am often successful at school.

Die Lehrer sind echt streng / sympathisch.
The teachers are really strict / nice.

Es gefällt mir (nicht), in die Schule zu gehen.
I (don't) like going to school.

Ich mag es (nicht), wenn Stunden ausfallen.
I (don't) like it when lessons are cancelled.

Ich finde den Schultag sehr anstrengend / abwechslungsreich.
I find the school day very tiring / varied.

Intensifiers

Use intensifiers to reinforce your opinion.

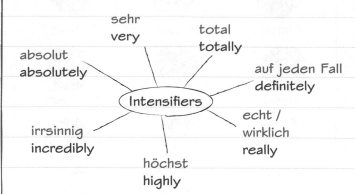

sehr — very
total — totally
absolut — absolutely
auf jeden Fall — definitely
irrsinnig — incredibly
echt / wirklich — really
höchst — highly

Ich finde Deutsch echt super.
I find German really great.

Spanisch ist sehr schwierig.
Spanish is very difficult.

Mein Lieblingsfach ist auf jeden Fall Werken.
My favourite subject is definitely DT.

In Geschichte habe ich absolut keine Probleme.
In history I have absolutely no problems.

Worked example

School

Beantworte diese Frage:

• Wie findest du deine Schule?

> Meiner Meinung nach ist Mathe sehr schwierig, besonders wenn man kein fleißiger Schüler ist. Ich finde Sport viel besser, weil wir nie Klassenarbeiten schreiben müssen.

Aiming higher

> Es ist absolut fair, dass Rauchen auf dem Schulgelände streng verboten ist, weil Rauchen sowieso schlecht für die Gesundheit ist. Die Schule kann sehr stressig sein. Wenn ich schlechte Noten bekomme, werde ich auch ein schlechtes Zeugnis bekommen, und dann werden meine Eltern sehr böse sein. In der Grundschule hatte man keine Prüfungen, keinen Stress.

Use the tips above to make sure you include plenty of variety in your speaking answers.

This student offers a couple of opinions and uses a **modal** with a conjunction, but it is all in the **present** tense.

Look at how this student uses a **variety** of elements and structures to give opinions about school:
- intensifiers
- present, future and past tenses
- modal verb
- **dass**, **weil** and **wenn** clauses.

Now try this

Now prepare to answer these questions as fully as you can.
• Wie findest du deine Schulfächer?
• Was war der beste Tag in der Schule letztes Jahr?
• Ist die Schule stressig für dich?
Try to speak for at least 30 seconds on each point.

School day

To understand and talk about a typical school day, you need a secure knowledge of times and days of the week. Make sure you have learnt them – see page 113.

Der Schultag

Die erste Stunde beginnt um zehn vor neun.
The first lesson starts at ten to nine.

Wir haben sechs Stunden pro Tag.
We have six lessons each day.

In der Pause gehen wir auf den Schulhof.
At break we go to the playground.

Wir essen zu Mittag in der Kantine.
We eat lunch in the canteen.

Man kann in der Bibliothek Hausaufgaben machen.
You can do homework in the library.

Nach der Schule gibt es ein gutes Angebot an AGs.
After school there is a good selection of clubs.

Sport haben wir immer als Doppelstunde.
We always have a double lesson for PE.

Linking words

Grammar page 92

These make your sentences longer and they **don't** change the word order!

| aber | but | oder | or |
| denn | because | und | and |

Man muss viel lernen und der Leistungsdruck ist enorm.
You have to learn a lot and the pressure to achieve is huge.

In der Pause plaudern wir oder wir machen Hausaufgaben.
At break we chat or we do homework.

Worked example

Stundenplan by Christine Nöstlinger
Read the extract from the text. It describes a girl's day at school.

Anika geht aus der Klasse. Sie geht zum Waschraum, der am weitesten von der 4a entfernt ist. Sie geht an Türen vorbei, hinter denen es still ist, an Türen, hinter denen eine Stimme zu hören ist. Sie erkennt die Stimmen. Eine Stimme mag sie. Die erste Stimme sagt: »… trat in die Dienste des Prinzen Karl August von Sachsen-Weimar …«

Es ist eine langsame Mitschreibestimme. »Sachsen-Weimar«, sagt die Stimme noch einmal, »Sachsen-Weimar«. Vorne, dort wo der Gang zur Treppe biegt, sind Schritte. Schnelle Schritte, Lehrerschritte. Schüler, die während der Unterrichtsstunde auf den Gängen sind, gehen nie so schnell.

Anika verschwindet im Waschraum.

Look at the example and read the text again.

Example: ☒ Anika leaves her classroom.

☐ **A** She goes to a class nearby.

☐ **B** The school is completely silent.

☐ **C** Anika hears different people.

☐ **D** One voice is teaching about a king.

☐ **E** Pupils should be copying details down.

☐ **F** Pupils are walking in the corridors.

☐ **G** Anika is not to be seen at the end.

Reading tips

- ✓ Don't ignore the example answer – it is there to help you get into the text.
- ✓ Anika hears something, so even if you don't know exactly what she heard (Stimme = voice), you still know statement **B** must be wrong.
- ✓ If you change your mind about your three answers, make sure you clearly **cross out** any answer you don't want.
- ✓ Put crosses in only **three** of the boxes.

Sometimes you have to **infer** meaning. The text says that pupils who walk in the corridors never go that quickly, so statement **F** cannot be correct.

Now try this

Now complete the activity on the left by putting a cross next to **three** more correct statements.

Types of schools

Make sure you are familiar with the German school system and types of schools, so you recognise a school if you hear or read about it!

Deutsche Schulen

Direktor (m) / Direktorin (f)	head teacher
Schulleiter (m) / Schulleiterin (f)	head teacher
Berufsschule (f)	vocational school
Gesamtschule (f)	comprehensive school
Grundschule (f)	primary school
Gymnasium (n)	grammar school
Hauptschule (f)	type of secondary school
Internat (n)	boarding school
Kindergarten (m)	pre-school
Privatschule (f)	private school
Realschule (f)	type of secondary school
Trimester / Semester (n)	term / semester
lernen	to learn
lehren / unterrichten	to teach
staatlich	state
gemischt	mixed

sich freuen auf + accusative

To talk about something you are looking forward to, use the verb sich freuen auf + the accusative case. So, if talking about school-related topics, you might say:

Ich freue mich (nicht) auf ...
I am (not) looking forward to ...

den Druck (m)	the pressure
die Klassenfahrt (f)	the school trip
das Schuljahr (n)	the school year
die Prüfungen (fpl)	the exams

Ich freue mich auf die Klassenfahrt.

Worked example

Deine Schule

Dein Freund schickt dir Fragen über deine Schule. Schreibe eine Antwort an ihn.
Du **musst** diesen Punkt einschließen:
Beschreibung von deiner Schule.

> Ich gehe auf eine Gesamtschule mit etwa tausend Schülern und Schülerinnen. Als ich in die siebte Klasse kam, war ich sehr nervös, weil das Schulgebäude einfach so groß und imposant war.

Aiming higher

> In der elften Klasse bin ich jetzt viel selbstbewusster und ich fange an, mich richtig auf die Oberstufe zu freuen. Hoffentlich werde ich bei den Prüfungen nicht durchfallen, damit ich nächstes Jahr das Abitur machen kann.

This extract is a good piece of writing, as it includes:
• present and past tense
• **als** + opinion + **weil** clause
• an interesting adjective (**imposant**).

Add some additional features to achieve the best possible response:
• inverted sentence
• comparative
• **anfangen** + **zu** + infinitive construction
• idiom **sich freuen auf**
• **hoffentlich** + future tense.

Now try this

Now include the following points and complete the above writing activity:
• worauf du dich in der Schule am meisten freust
• wie du in der siebten Klasse warst
• welche Pläne du für das nächste Trimester hast.
Schreibe ungefähr 80–90 Wörter **auf Deutsch**.

School facilities

Familiarise yourself with the rooms in a school so you can be specific in a description.

Das Schulgelände

Aula (f)	school hall
Bibliothek (f)	library
Computerraum (m)	computer room
Gang (m)	corridor
Kantine (f)	canteen
Klassenzimmer (n)	classroom
Labor (n)	laboratory
Lehrerzimmer (n)	staffroom
Schulhof (m)	playground
Sekretariat (n)	office
Sporthalle (f)	sports hall
Toiletten (fpl)	toilets
gut / schlecht ausgestattet	well / badly equipped
modern / altmodisch	modern / old-fashioned
neu gebaut	newly built

Relative pronouns

Relative pronouns translate as 'who', 'that', 'which'. They agree with the noun they are referring to and send the verb to the end of the clause.

Hier ist ein Schüler, der (m) auf den Bildschirm starrt.
Here is a pupil who is staring at the screen.

Hier ist eine Schülerin, die (f) einen Schal trägt.
Here is a pupil who is wearing a scarf.

Hier ist ein Klassenzimmer, das (n) altmodisch ist.
Here is a classroom that is old-fashioned.

Dort sind die Toiletten, die (pl) immer sauber sind.
There are the toilets, which are always clean.

Describing a photo

- ✓ Give your opinion of the photo, saying what you think of the room pictured. Don't just identify it as a computer room.
- ✓ Compare the room to your school, saying whether you have lessons in a computer room and, if so, which ones and when.
- ✓ Try to use a different verb in each sentence to add variety to your work.

Worked example

In the classroom

Schau dir das Foto an und sei bereit, über Folgendes zu sprechen:

- Beschreibung des Fotos.

Aiming higher

Hier ist ein Foto von einer Schulklasse beim Unterricht im Computerraum. In dieser Reihe sitzen vier Schüler am Computer und schauen sich den Bildschirm an. Im Hintergrund sehe ich einen Lehrer, der die Klasse beobachtet. In der Mitte gibt es einen Jungen, der ein rotes T-Shirt trägt und neben ihm merke ich einen anderen Jungen, der etwas auf der Tastatur tippt.

Describing a photo is a great opportunity to use relative pronouns to help your work flow better.

Now try this

Now prepare to talk on the subject of these bullet points as fully as you can:
- Ob deine Schule gut ausgestattet ist.
- Die beste Schulstunde, die du je gehabt hast.
- Was du an deiner Schule ändern möchtest.
- !
Try to speak for at least 30 seconds on each point.

At Higher level, you need to answer an unexpected question at the end of your description. Be ready to listen to the question and answer it accordingly!

School rules

Use modal verbs müssen (to have to) and dürfen (to be allowed to) with an infinitive verb when talking about rules at school – or at home.

Die Schulordnung

Die Regeln sind total ...
The rules are totally ...

(un)fair / (un)gerecht.	(un)fair.
dumm / blöd.	stupid.
nervig / ärgerlich.	annoying.
Strafarbeit (f)	lines, detention
nachsitzen	to have a detention

Man muss ...   You have to ...

die Hausaufgaben machen.	do the homework.
im Klassenzimmer ruhig sein.	be quiet in class.
den Müll trennen.	sort the rubbish.

Man darf nicht rauchen.
You are not allowed to smoke.
Man darf die Stunden nicht schwänzen.
You are not allowed to skip lessons.

Man darf keine ...   You are not allowed to ...

Kopfhörer im Unterricht tragen.
wear headphones in lessons.
Sportschuhe in der Schule tragen.
wear trainers to school.

Using müssen (to have to)

Grammar page 98

Müssen is a modal verb, so it needs an infinitive:
Man muss Hausaufgaben machen.
You have to do homework.

Man muss ... You have to ...	höflich sein. be polite.
	viel üben, um ein Instrument zu spielen. practise a lot to play an instrument.
	sich ordentlich anziehen. dress smartly.
	sitzen bleiben. repeat a school year.

Translating into English

✓ Make sure you have learnt plenty of vocabulary across all the topics before the exam – that way translations like this will be much easier.

✓ Don't ignore qualifiers and words such as mindestens – they all need to be translated.

✓ Look for word families to help you understand unfamiliar vocabulary: mindestens is linked to Minderheit (minority).

✓ Use common sense – the two pencil case items are the basic equipment needed, so they are unlikely to be a fountain pen and a protractor.

✓ If you come across a conjunction, such as wo or weil, look to the end of the clause to find the accompanying verb(s).

Worked example

Translation

Translate this passage **into English**.   **(2 marks)**

> Ich besuche eine Schule wo die Schulordnung total dumm ist, weil man mindestens einen Bleistift und ein Lineal im Etui haben muss.

I go to a school where the rules are really stupid, because you have to have at least a pencil and a ruler in your pencil case.

Note how the English translation of **die Schulordnung ... ist** becomes 'the rules are'. Translating means using English terms, and not just doing a word-for-word translation: 'the school order ... is' does not make sense.

Now try this

Now complete the translation.   **(5 marks)**

> Letztes Trimester hat ein Schüler auf dem Schulhof geraucht, weil er das cool gefunden hat. Der Direktor war aber sehr böse und hat den Jungen sofort nach Hause geschickt. Ich würde in der Schule nie rauchen oder Alkohol trinken, weil ich keine Strafarbeit bekommen möchte.

Pressures at school

Learn a few key phrases to talk about problems and pressures at school.

Der Schulstress

Elternsprechabend (m)	parents' evening
Note (f)	grade
Zeugnis (n)	report
Angst vor den Noten haben	

to be anxious about the grades

das Jahr wiederholen	to repeat the year
sitzenbleiben	to repeat a year
durchfallen	to fail (an exam)

Die Prüfungen finde ich stressig.
I find exams stressful.
Wir stehen unter großem Leistungsdruck.
We are under a lot of pressure to achieve.
Viele Schüler leiden unter Schulstress.
Many pupils suffer from stress at school.
Ich bin oft abwesend, weil es mir schlecht
 geht. I am often absent because I feel ill.
Die Lehrer fehlen oft, weil sie gestresst
 sind. The teachers are often absent
 because they are stressed.

Obwohl

Grammar page 93

Obwohl (although) is a subordinating conjunction which sends the verb to the end of the clause, like weil.
Obwohl es eine kleine Schule ist, gibt
 es hier viele AGs.
Although it is a small school, there are
 lots of clubs here.
Er ist zur Schule gegangen, obwohl er
 schreckliche Kopfschmerzen hatte.
He went to school, although he had a
 terrible headache.

Wir müssen zu viele Klassenarbeiten schreiben.
We have to do too many tests.

Worked example

Schule
Übersetze **ins Deutsche**.

> Today there is great pressure to achieve at school. In the past you could go to school to enjoy lessons and play with your friends.

 Aiming higher

> Heute gibt es großen Leistungsdruck in der Schule. In der Vergangenheit konnte man zur Schule gehen, um den Unterricht zu genießen und mit Freunden zu spielen.

Translating into German

✓ Grammar is the key to translations into German, so make sure you are confident with verbs and pronouns in the main tenses: present, past, future and conditional form.

✓ Get your word order right – unless there is a subordinating conjunction (e.g. dass), the verb has to come in second place.

For the highest marks, you have to show you can use subordinating conjunctions, such as **weil**, **um ... zu** and **obwohl** with a variety of tenses.

Exam alert

Although the first sentence in a translation might appear 'easy', make sure you don't slip up with a silly mistake: check the tense, word order and any adjective agreements before you move on to the more challenging second sentence.

Now try this

Now complete the translation **into German**.

> Although pupils have to do tests frequently these days, we can still really look forward to class trips. If I study hard to get good grades, I may also perhaps get a reward from my parents – and that will be worth it!

Primary school

Talking about your primary school offers a great opportunity to use the imperfect tense.

School equipment

Bleistift (m)   Etui (n)   Filzstift (m)

Füller (m)   Heft (n)   Klebstoff (m)

Kuli / Kugelschreiber (m)   Lineal (n)   Radiergummi (m)

Schere (f)   Schreibblock (m)   Spitzer (m)

Taschenrechner (m)   Wörterbuch (n)

Modals – imperfect tense

> **Grammar page 99**

kann – can	➡	konnte – could
muss – have to	➡	musste – had to
darf – am allowed	➡	durfte – was allowed
will – want	➡	wollte – wanted
soll – am supposed to	➡	sollte – should
mag – like	➡	mochte – liked

In der Grundschule ... At primary school ...	konnte ich kein Französisch sprechen. I couldn't speak French.
	musste ich mit meiner Mutter zur Schule gehen. I had to go to school with my mum.
	durfte ich kein Handy haben. I wasn't allowed a mobile.

Using an imperfect modal is a good indicator that you are aiming high.

Worked example

 READING

At primary school

Read the text.
The writer remembers childhood family life.

> In der Grundschule habe ich mich immer gut benommen, aber Tim wollte nie machen, was von ihm verlangt wurde. Meine Eltern sagten Tim, dass er mehr wie ich sein sollte. Wenn ich etwas Dummes machte, lachte mein Vater immer, aber mit Tim war er immer böse.

Exam alert

For this task, good comprehension skills are needed, as well as an ability to draw conclusions from the text. The questions are not phrased in exactly the same way as they appear in the text, so be careful!

Put a cross ✗ in the correct box.
Example: When Tim was younger, he ...

☒ **A** was not very obedient at school

☐ **B** was a well-behaved pupil

☐ **C** did not go to primary school

☐ **D** was just like his brother

Now try this

  READING

Read the text again and put a cross ✗ in the correct box.

Their dad reacted to Tim and his brother ...

☐ **A** proudly

☐ **B** in the same way

☐ **C** in different ways

☐ **D** negatively

Success at school

Talking about success at school can cover other topic areas – look at sport and volunteering for ideas of success at school.

Wir feiern!

Erfolg (m)	success
Leistung (f)	achievement
Erfolg feiern	to celebrate success
gratulieren	to congratulate
begabt	gifted, talented
erfolgreich	successful
gut in der Klasse aufpassen	to pay attention in class
ein gutes Zeugnis bekommen	to get a good report
Fortschritte machen	to make progress
die Prüfung bestehen	to pass the exam
einen Preis gewinnen	to win a prize
den zweiten Platz erreichen	to achieve second place

Dative verb gelingen (to succeed)

The dative verb *gelingen* works in the same way as *gefallen* (to like): *es gefällt mir* (I like it).

Es gelingt mir, die beste Note in der Klasse zu bekommen. I succeed in getting the best grade in the class.

Gestern ist es mir gelungen, einen Preis zu gewinnen.
Yesterday I succeeded in winning a prize.

Es gelingt …

mir	(me)	uns	(us)		
dir	(you)	euch	(you – pl)		
ihm	(him)	ihnen / Ihnen	(them / you –		
ihr	(her)		polite)		

Es ist mir gelungen, das Abitur zu bestehen! I succeeded in passing my A levels!

 Worked example

Prize day interview

Your penfriend Sonja has sent you a podcast of her interview as a school prize winner.

(a) Listen to the interview and put a cross ✗ in the correct box.

Example: Sonja …

- ☐ **A** finds her prize really unimportant
- ☒ **B** wants to achieve more
- ☐ **C** is satisfied with her level of achievement
- ☐ **D** can't concentrate on her exams

Listen to the recording

Recycle useful expressions you come across in audioscripts in your speaking and writing tasks:
der Höhepunkt – highlight
ohne Zweifel – without doubt
ehrlich gesagt – to be honest

— Sonja, du hast den ersten Preis für Leistungen an der Schule gewonnen, nicht? War das für dich der Höhepunkt an der Schule?

— Ein Höhepunkt war das ohne Zweifel, aber ehrlich gesagt ist es mir wichtiger, jetzt noch fleißiger zu arbeiten, um noch bessere Leistungen zu erreichen. Nächstes Jahr hoffe ich, in die Oberstufe zu kommen, also muss ich mich auf die Prüfungen konzentrieren.

 Now try this

Now listen to the next part of the interview and put a cross ✗ in the correct box.

Listen to the recording

(b) Sonja …
- ☐ **A** met the mayor at primary school.
- ☐ **B** had her photo taken with the mayor.
- ☐ **C** took part in a competition at secondary school.
- ☐ **D** is unhappy that her photo can be found online.

(1 mark)

You need to infer the answer here – it isn't going to be spelled out for you!

Class trips

German, Swiss and Austrian schools all organise annual class trips, so you may come across one in your exams!

Die Klassenfahrt

einmal im Schuljahr once in a school year
mit der Klasse wegfahren
to go away with the class
einander besser kennenlernen
to get to know each other better
miteinander gut / schlecht auskommen
to get on well / badly with each other
neue Sportarten ausprobieren
to try new sports

Erfahrungen sammeln	to collect experiences
Wanderwoche (f)	walking week
Wochenprogramm (n)	week's agenda
im Wald	in the forest
in den Bergen	in the mountains
im Freien	in the outdoors
Heimweh haben	to be homesick

ein positives / negatives Erlebnis
a positive / negative experience

Giving your opinion

Make it clear when you are giving an opinion rather than stating a fact.

Ich	finde, denke, meine, glaube,	Klassenfahrten sind super. das Wochenprogramm ist interessant. das wird eine positive Erfahrung sein.

For a reminder of how to use Ich finde, dass + verb to the end, see 'Opinions' on page 39.

Wir lieben die Klassenfahrt im Wald! We love the class trip in the forest!

Worked example

School trip

Sei bereit, über Folgendes zu sprechen:

- Ob eine Klassenfahrt immer positiv ist?

> Meiner Meinung nach machen Klassenfahrten immer viel Spaß, weil man eine Woche weg von der Schule und den Eltern verbringt.
> Letztes Jahr bin ich auf Klassenfahrt nach Leipzig gefahren und das war ein wunderbares Erlebnis.

Aiming higher

> Das Wochenprogramm war besonders interessant, weil wir jeden Tag etwas Neues unternommen haben. Am Ende des Tages waren wir so erschöpft, dass wir sofort eingeschlafen sind. Ich stelle mir vor, die Lehrer waren darüber besonders zufrieden.

This student has included the conjunctions **weil** and **so ... dass**, as well as an infinitive verb construction: **ich stelle mir vor, ...**

Exam alert

Read every word on the exam card – words like **immer** (always) are important.

If there is an **ob** at the start of a question, it is asking you 'whether' the statement is true: here, whether a class trip is always positive, or not.

Give your opinion using a phrase such as **meiner Meinung nach** + verb next. A great way to start!

Don't hang around in the present tense for too long, but move your conversation along by talking about a related experience you **had** in the past.

Now try this

Now prepare to answer the question in the worked example as fully as you can. Try to speak for at least 30 seconds.

School exchange

You will have to ask one (Foundation) or two (Higher) questions in the role play section of the Speaking exam – make sure you are confident with doing just that.

Asking questions in two ways

1 With a question word – see page 8 for a longer list:

Wo?	Where?
Wer?	Who?
Was?	What?

2 By inverting a sentence:

Wir treffen uns. ➡ Treffen wir uns?

Du fährst auf Austausch. ➡ Fährst du auf Austausch?

Auf Austausch

Austauschpartner (m) / Austauschpartnerin (f)	exchange partner
Austauschschule (f)	exchange school
Besuch (m)	visit
Brieffreund (m) / Brieffreundin (f)	penfriend
Gastfamilie (f)	host family
zu Besuch sein	to be visiting
gut / schlecht miteinander auskommen	to get on well / badly with each other
Tagesausflüge machen	to go on day trips
die Sehenswürdigkeiten besichtigen	to go sightseeing
Die Tagesroutine hat mir (nicht) gefallen.	I liked (didn't like) the daily routine.
Das Essen hat mir (nicht) geschmeckt.	I liked (didn't like) the food.
Die Woche war ein großer Erfolg.	The week was a big success.
Ich möchte wieder dorthin fahren.	I would like to go there again.

Worked example

Instructions to candidate: You are on the German school exchange. You meet up with your exchange partner. Your teacher will play the part of your exchange partner and will speak first.

Task

Ich bin dein Austauschpartner / deine Austauschpartnerin und wir treffen uns in der Mittagspause an der Schule in Deutschland.

1 Schule – Meinung und Grund

– Hallo, wie findest du es hier in der Schule?
– Es gefällt mir hier gut, weil man keine Uniform tragen muss.

2 Meinung zum Schultag

– Wie findest du den Schultag bei uns?
– Die Schule beginnt zu früh, denke ich, aber es freut mich, dass man nachmittags nicht in der Schule ist.

3 !

– Wie hast du die letzte Stunde gefunden?
– Englisch war sehr einfach, habe ich gedacht.

Exam alert

Get the register right – here, you are talking to somebody the same age as you, so use **du**.

Two pieces of information required here (opinion + reason) = two pieces communicated. Job done!

The student has prepared this answer in the preparation time – this makes the prompt easier to tackle.

A straightforward reply is required here – no need to embellish it but just ensure you respond accurately, using the correct tense: here, past.

Now try this

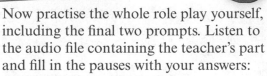

Now practise the whole role play yourself, including the final two prompts. Listen to the audio file containing the teacher's part and fill in the pauses with your answers:

Listen to the recording

4 ? Pläne – heute Nachmittag

5 ? Schlafen – wann

School events

Make sure you know about lots of different activities that go on at school – competitions, productions, concerts, sport, festivals and so on.

Schulveranstaltungen

in der Theatergruppe sein
to be in the drama club
die Schülerzeitung produzieren
to produce the school newspaper
an einem Wettbewerb teilnehmen
to take part in a competition
beim Lesefest mitmachen
to take part in the reading festival
im Orchester mitspielen
to play in the orchestra
an einer Debatte teilnehmen
to take part in a debate
Mitglied der Mannschaft sein
to be a member of the team
Die Veranstaltung wird in der Bibliothek stattfinden.
The event will take place in the library.
Interessierst du dich für den Kuchenverkauf?
Are you interested in the cake sale?

Verbs with prepositions

Some verbs are always followed by a preposition, so learn the parts together.

- Some take the accusative case:
  sich konzentrieren auf   to concentrate on
  sich interessieren für   to be interested in
  Ich muss mich auf die Kunstausstellung konzentrieren.
  I must concentrate on the art exhibition.

- And some take the dative case:
  Angst vor ... haben   to be anxious about
  teilnehmen an   to take part in

Ich habe Angst vor dem Schulfußballspiel.
I am anxious about the school football match.

Worked example

School competition

You hear an interview on school radio about a competition. What is said?

(a) Choose the **two** correct answers.

Listen to the recording

Example: ☒ The competition was a great success.

☐ **A** The competition was a disaster.
☐ **B** The competition is new.
☐ **C** The first play was unusual.
☐ **D** The cast were not very good.
☐ **E** The competition was a great success.

(2 marks)

— Gestern Abend hat der Theaterwettbewerb unter großem Applaus in der Aula stattgefunden. Seit fünf Jahren läuft jetzt diese beliebte Veranstaltung und dieses Jahr waren die Theaterproduktionen besser als je zuvor!

Parts of words can lead you to the meaning – here, **je zuvor** is related to **vor** (before) and means 'ever before'.

Now try this

Now listen to the rest of the recording so that you can complete activity **(a)** on the left and do activity **(b)** below.

Listen to the recording

(b) Choose the **two** correct answers.

☐ **A** Class 8 performed an old-fashioned piece.
☐ **B** Their outfits were impressive.
☐ **C** The play was a bit ordinary.
☐ **D** The play was well received.
☐ **E** The audience were not very impressed.
☐ **F** The audience were mainly parents.

(2 marks)

The fact that the competition happened **unter großem Applaus** indicates that it was a success. The recording is not going to spell out to you 'it was a success' – you have to glean this from the context of the piece.

Future study

Talking about future plans enables you to say what you **want** to do over the next few years.

Sich weiterbilden

Ich möchte / werde ...	I would like to / will ...
in die Oberstufe gehen.	go into the sixth form.
einen Studienplatz bekommen.	get a college place.
auf die Uni(versität) gehen.	go to uni(versity).
die Prüfungen wiederholen.	retake the exams.
in die Weiterbildung gehen.	do further education.
(Wirtschaftslehre) studieren.	study (economics).
Mittlere Reife (f)	GCSE equivalent
Abitur (Abi) (n)	A level equivalent
Abiturient (m) / Abiturientin (f)	person doing the 'Abitur'
Student (m) / Studentin (f)	student (uni)
Abschlussprüfung (f)	school leaving exam
Schulabschluss (m)	school leaving certificate
Hochschulabschluss (m)	degree
Hochschulbildung (f)	higher education
Berufsberater (m)	careers adviser
Kurs (m)	course
Resultat / Ergebnis (n)	result
Qualifikation (f)	qualification

Using wollen (to want to)

Grammar page 98

Wollen is a modal verb, so it needs an infinitive.

Ich will in die Oberstufe gehen.
I want to go into the sixth form.

Don't confuse the German will (meaning 'want to') with the English 'will' (future intent).

Ich will ...	weiterbilden.
	carry on studying.
I want to ...	auf die Universität gehen.
	go to university.
	eine Lehre machen.
	do an apprenticeship.
	an der Uni Englisch und Geschichte studieren.
	study English and history at university.

Worked example

Nächstes Jahr

Beantworte diese Frage:

• Was möchtest du nächstes Jahr machen?

Gleich nach den Prüfungen will ich ein Wochenende mit meiner Clique an der Küste verbringen. Ich freue mich irrsinnig darauf, obwohl meine Eltern nicht so begeistert darüber sind. Nächstes Trimester werde ich hoffentlich in die Oberstufe kommen, wenn ich die notwendigen Noten bekomme. Ich will Fremdsprachen und Mathe lernen, weil ich eines Tages gern im Ausland arbeiten möchte.

Exam alert

You will need to speak on both your prepared and unprepared conversation topics for an equal amount of time, so have plenty of practice conversations in advance to prepare.

Avoid long pauses by using fillers such as **Moment mal, Tja, Wie ich (schon) gesagt habe, Zum Beispiel.**

Aiming higher

✓ Go for **quality** not quantity. Allow plenty of time for interaction to show that you can understand and respond to what the teacher says.

✓ You will get no credit for repeating language from other parts of your Speaking exam, so make sure you have a solid supply of **language** across **all topic areas**.

Now try this

Now prepare to answer the following questions and speak for one minute without **hesitating** or **repeating** yourself!

• Warum sind Pläne dir wichtig oder nicht wichtig?

• Welche Pläne hattest du in der Grundschule?

• Warum können sich Pläne oft ändern?

Record yourself and listen back to hear how German you sound.

Jobs

Make sure you know both the male and female versions of the jobs listed below.

Arbeit

Angestellter (m) / Angestellte (f)	employee
Arbeitgeber/in	employer
Bäcker/in	baker
Bauarbeiter/in	builder
Bauer (m) / Bäuerin (f)	farmer
Elektriker/in	electrician
Fahrer/in	driver
Fleischer/in / Metzger/in	butcher
Flugbegleiter/in	cabin crew
Kassierer/in	cashier
Kellner/in	waiter / waitress
Klempner/in	plumber
Mechaniker/in	mechanic
Modeschöpfer/in	fashion designer
Techniker/in	technician
Tischler/in	carpenter / joiner
Vertreter/in	sales rep

Mein Bruder arbeitet in der Schneiderei.
My brother works in tailoring.

gut / schlecht bezahlt   well / badly paid

Saying 'somebody' and 'nobody'

jemand – somebody
Jemand arbeitet in der Metzgerei.
Somebody is working in the butcher's.

niemand – nobody
Niemand arbeitet auf dem Bauernhof.
Nobody is working at the farm.

accusative = für jemanden / niemanden
dative = mit jemandem / niemandem

Worked example

LISTENING TRACK 40

Social media

Your German penfriend, Leon, has sent you a podcast.

Listen to his podcast and answer the following question **in English**.

(a) How many sisters does Leon have?   **(1 mark)**
    2 sisters

> – Ich stelle dir meine Familie vor. Meine ältere Schwester arbeitet als Vertreterin bei einer Techno-Firma und spielt gern Tennis in ihrer Freizeit. Meine andere Schwester heißt Carmen und sie ist nervig.

Listening tips
☑ Read the questions **before** you listen.
☑ Watch out for questions requiring **two** pieces of information.
☑ If the answers are supposed to be **in English**, jotting down words in German won't help you!

You have to wait some time to get the answer to the first question. Don't jump to the conclusion that Leon only has one sister. Carry on listening and you will hear him mention **eine andere Schwester** (another sister).

Question (d) asks for two pieces of information – make sure you give both of them.

Now try this

LISTENING TRACK 41

Now listen to the rest of the recording and answer the following questions **in English**.
(b) What are Carmen's job plans? Give **one** detail.   **(1 mark)**
(c) How do we know that Leon's mother works hard?   **(1 mark)**
(d) What is unusual about his father? Give **two** details.   **(2 marks)**

Professions

Use strategies to help you when translating into English – does the German word look like an English word?

Berufe

Apotheker/in	pharmacist
Architekt/in	architect
Arzt (m) / Ärztin (f)	doctor
Beamter (m) / Beamtin (f)	civil servant
Dichter/in	poet
Feuerwehrmann (m) / Feuerwehrfrau (f)	firefighter
Informatiker/in	computer scientist
Ingenieur/in	engineer
Journalist/in	journalist
Krankenpfleger (m) / Krankenschwester (f)	nurse
Künstler/in	artist
Lehrer/in	teacher
Manager/in	manager
Mechaniker/in	mechanic
Polizist/in	police officer
Schauspieler/in	actor
Zahnarzt (m) / Zahnärztin (f)	dentist

Ich habe viel Ehrgeiz / Ich bin ehrgeizig.
I am ambitious.

Man muss oft in Besprechungen sitzen.
You have to sit in meetings a lot.

Imperfect subjunctive modals

Impress with these expressions in the Speaking exam. They are no more complicated than modals in the present tense, but they will improve your speaking and writing!

Ich möchte Tierärztin werden.
I would like to become a vet.

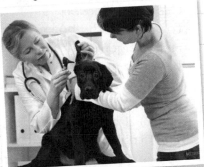

Note that in German the word for 'a' is not needed before the job.

Du könntest viel Geld verdienen.
You could earn lots of money.

Du solltest versuchen, Arzt zu werden.
You should try to become a doctor.

Translating into English

- ✓ Use words that look like their English equivalent to help with translations.
- ✓ Don't switch tenses when you are translating – arbeitet is present tense: 'works'.
- ✓ Krankenhaus is linked to krank (ill), so what do you think an 'ill house' is?
- ✓ Connect words – if you can't remember what Ärztin is, can you recall the male term Arzt? Think logically about where this person works, the Krankenhaus. Who works there?

Worked example

Translation

Translate this passage **into English**.

> Meine Mutter arbeitet als Ärztin. Um sechs Uhr fährt sie immer zum Krankenhaus.

My mother works as a doctor. At six o'clock she always drives to the hospital.

(3 marks)

Now try this

Now complete the translation.

> Letztes Wochenende hat sie hart gearbeitet. Nächstes Jahr wird sie sich um einen neuen Job bewerben.

(4 marks)

Job wishes

Use this page to learn some high level language about your wishes for a future job.

Berufswünsche

Ich hoffe, ...   I hope ...

bei einer globalen Firma zu arbeiten.
to work for a global company.

ein hohes Gehalt zu verdienen.
to earn a high wage.

Chef/in zu werden.
to become the boss.

meine eigene Firma zu gründen.
to found my own company.

(nicht) in einer Fabrik zu arbeiten.
(not) to work in a factory.

(nicht) draußen / im Freien zu arbeiten.
(not) to work outside.

von zu Hause aus zu arbeiten.
to work from home.

gute Aufstiegsmöglichkeiten zu haben.
to have good chances of promotion.

im Ausland zu arbeiten.   to work abroad.

Teilzeit zu arbeiten.   to work part-time.

in der Sportabteilung / Musikindustrie zu arbeiten.
to work in the sports sector / music industry.

Infinitive expressions

Grammar
page 94

Ich	hoffe, ... (hope)	+ zu + infinitive.
	versuche, ... (try)	
	habe vor, ... (intend)	

Ich habe vor, ins Ausland zu reisen.
I intend to travel abroad.

Ich hoffe, viel Geld zu verdienen.
I hope to earn lots of money.

Ich fange an / beginne, an die Zukunft zu denken.
I am beginning to think about the future.

Ich versuche, einen Teilzeitjob zu finden.
I am trying to find a part-time job.

Selecting correct words

✓ The question here gives you an idea of the content and helps you to be ready for the dialogue.

✓ Make sure you read through the gapped sentences before you listen – the recording is short and every word counts, so really concentrate once the audio starts.

✓ You only need to use **four** of the words from the box, so watch out for distractors.

Worked example

LISTENING TRACK 42

Listen to the recording

Job wishes
Lothar and Markus are talking about their job wishes.
What are they looking for?
Complete the sentences. Use the correct words from the box.

(a) Lothar is looking for ...excitement... and ....
(1 mark)

(b) Markus is looking for .... and ....
(2 marks)

travel	routine
excitement	courses
variety	promotion
salary	accommodation

– Was findest du wichtig für deinen Beruf, Lothar?

– Routine ist nichts für mich. Ich suche etwas Spannendes. Am liebsten würde ich Feuerwehrmann werden, weil man jeden Tag etwas anderes macht.

Exam alert

Don't be put off by extra letters at the end of familiar words: **spannend** = exciting, **etwas Spannendes** = something exciting.

Now try this

LISTENING TRACK 43

Listen to the recording

Now listen to the rest of the recording and complete the activity on the left.

Make sure you are aware of words that go together, such as **Geld** (money) and **das Gehalt** (salary).

Opinions about jobs

The opinions on this page can equally well be applied to other topic areas – holidays, school, visits.

Meinungen über die Arbeit

Arbeitsbedingungen (pl)   work conditions

Ich habe ein sehr positives Gefühl.	I have a very positive feeling.
Es war mein Traum, diesen Job zu bekommen.	It was my dream to get this job.
Ich fühle mich auf der Arbeit wohl.	I feel comfortable at work.
Der Job ist ein großer Erfolg.	The job is a big success.
Es ist das Beste für mich.	It is the best for me.
Das ist ein ausgezeichnetes Erlebnis.	That is an excellent experience.
Ich wäre gern noch länger geblieben.	I would have liked to stay longer.

Dieser Job würde mich ärgern.	This job would annoy me.
Das ist so ein Pech, kein Gehalt zu bekommen.	That is such bad luck not to get a salary.
Ich wünsche mir keine schlecht bezahlte Stelle.	I don't wish for a badly paid position.
Es wäre eine große Enttäuschung.	It would be a big disappointment.
Ich würde es niemandem empfehlen.	I would not recommend it to anyone.
Ich würde das vermeiden.	I would avoid that.

Giving opinions

Use the following to express an opinion:

Meiner Meinung nach sind die Arbeitsbedingungen prima.

In my opinion the terms and conditions are excellent.

Other words for 'to think':

finden   denken

meinen   glauben

Remember that after dass the verb goes to the end of the clause, as with wo and weil:

Ich finde, dass manche Arbeitgeber gemein sind. I think that some employers are mean.

Es gefällt mir, dass es eine Kantine für die Mittagspause gibt.

I am pleased that there is a canteen for lunch break.

Opinions practice

You may need to identify whether an opinion is **positive**, **negative** or both **positive and negative**, so practise with this activity.

LISTENING TRACK 44

Listen to the recording

	☺	☹	☺☹
1	X		

– Ich finde, die neue Stelle ist ein großer Erfolg und macht mir besonders Spaß.

Understanding opinions

☑ Listening activities often rely on you understanding the **opinion** given, so always listen for clues, such as the speaker's **intonation**, to help you identify whether they are being **positive** or **negative**.

☑ Also listen out for the opinion words above to alert you to the fact it is an **opinion** and not a **fact**.

☑ You will also come across **opinions** in the Writing, Speaking and Reading papers, so make sure you are full of opinion knowledge!

Lots of positive words here plus a happy-sounding speaker point you to the answer: positive.

Now try this

LISTENING TRACK 45

Now listen to the remaining **nine** opinions. Decide whether they are **positive**, **negative** or both **positive and negative**.

Listen to the recording

Watch out for the word **Probleme** in no. 4. Here, it is linked with **trotz** (despite), so maybe it is a positive opinion after all?

Job adverts

Make sure you're prepared with this vocabulary connected with job seeking.

Stellenangebote

Arbeitsbedingungen (pl)	work conditions
Arbeitsstunden (pl)	hours of work
Aufstiegsmöglichkeiten (pl)	chances of promotion
Euro pro Stunde	euros per hour
Kollege (m) / Kollegin (f)	colleague
Mitarbeiter (m) / Mitarbeiterin (f)	co-worker
Stelle (f) / Job (m)	job
Stellenangebote (pl)	job vacancies
Stellenanzeige (f)	job advert
Termin (m)	appointment
ausgebildet	qualified, educated
erfahren	experienced
qualifiziert	qualified
teamfähig	good team worker
verantwortlich	responsible

Genitive prepositions

The following all take the genitive case:

außerhalb	outside, beyond
statt	instead of
trotz	despite
während	during
wegen	due to, because of

(m) der Anruf – statt des Anrufs
(der ➡ des + -s) instead of the call

(f) die Pause – während der Pause
(die ➡ der) during the break

(n) das Gehalt – trotz des niedrigen Gehalts
(das ➡ des + -s) despite the low salary

(pl) die Arbeitsstunden – wegen der Arbeitsstunden
(die ➡ der) due to the working hours

To show possession, use the following:
der Job meines Vaters – my father's job
der Chef der Firma – the firm's boss
der Bruder meiner Tante – my aunt's brother
das Ziel der Kinder – the children's aim

Der Job eines Arbeitsuchenden ist schwierig!
The work of a job seeker is hard!

Worked example

 WRITING

Stellensuche
Übersetze **ins Deutsche**.

(a) I am looking for a job.   **(2 marks)**
<u>Ich suche eine Stelle.</u>

You do not need a word for 'for' in this translation, as **suchen** means 'to look for'.

eine Stelle = ein Job / eine Arbeit
ein Freund / eine Freundin = ein Bekannter / eine Bekannte

Translating into German

☑ German nouns need **capital** letters!

☑ Look at **who** you are writing about in each sentence – yourself? Another person? More than one person? You need to have the correct part of the verb to match.

☑ Look at **when** you are writing about – is it something happening now (present tense) or a past action (past tense)?

You need to make sure your translated sentences flow and make sense. Leave yourself time to read them through to double check.

Now try this

 WRITING

Now translate these sentences **into German**.
(b) My friend earns two euros per hour.   **(2 marks)**
(c) He works in an office in the town centre.   **(2 marks)**
(d) Last year I worked as a waiter.   **(3 marks)**
(e) I need a job because I have no money.   **(3 marks)**

If you can't recall a specific German word, work around it, making sure you convey the same meaning; for example, 'I worked' could equally well be expressed as 'I had a job'.

Applying for a job

Make sure you are familiar with letter-writing conventions.

Sich um einen Job bewerben

einen Bewerbungsbrief schreiben
to write a letter of application
das Bewerbungsformular ausfüllen
to fill in the application form
Ich interessiere mich für den Job ...
I am interested in the job ...
  als Küchenhilfe.   as kitchen staff.
  als Kellner/in.   as a waiter / waitress.
  im Schwimmbad.   at the swimming pool.
Ich habe ausgezeichnete Sprachkenntnisse.
I have excellent language skills.
Ich möchte vom Juli bis September arbeiten.
I would like to work from July to September.
Anbei finden Sie meinen Lebenslauf.
Please find my CV enclosed.

Writing a formal letter

Sehr geehrter Herr X	Dear Mr X
Sehr geehrte Frau Y	Dear Mrs Y
zu Händen von Z	for the attention of Z
in Bezug auf	further to / following
Rufen Sie mich an.	Call me.
Vielen Dank im Voraus	Many thanks in advance
Mit bestem Gruß	With best wishes
Mit freundlichen Grüßen	Yours sincerely
Alles Gute	All the best

Exam alert

Tasks like these can be deceptively tricky. If you didn't know the meaning of **wieder einmal** (once again), this question would trip you up! Knowing key vocabulary is essential.

Worked example

Wieder keine Arbeit by **Wilfried's Ernst**

Read the extract from the text.
Wilfried's is on his way to the job centre.
Put a cross ✗ in the correct box.

Example: Why is Wilfried's going to the job centre?

☐ **A** looking for his first job
☒ **B** had to leave his previous job
☐ **C** wants a long-term job
☐ **D** meeting friends there

Ich muss heute zum Arbeitsamt gehen. Leider habe ich gestern schon wieder einmal meinen Job verloren. Das passiert mir leider häufig.

Es ist wie ein Spiel: ich finde einen Arbeitsplatz, den ich tolerieren kann. Ich suche aber immer noch etwas Interessanteres. Diese Stelle mache ich nur bis den Tag, wann etwas Besseres erscheint.

Diesmal arbeitete ich in der Jackenabteilung eines berühmten Kaufhauses. Ich musste viel herumstehen, die Kunden begrüßen und endlose Jacken richtig aufhängen. Nach einigen Tagen langweilte ich mich so sehr, dass ich mir für meine Kollegen Spitznamen ausdachte. Ich weiß nicht, wie ich auf die *Fix und Foxi* Zeichentrickfilmcharaktere kam, doch ich teilte jedem Mitarbeiter je nach Charakter eine Figur aus diesem Comicheft zu.

Reading tips

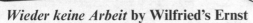

✓ Don't expect to understand everything word for word and be prepared for vocabulary from a variety of topics: jobs, clothes, shopping and personality all come up here.

Now try this

Now read the extract again and complete the reading activity.

(a) What sort of job has Karl's always looked for? **(1 mark)**
☐ **A** temporary   ☐ **B** more interesting   ☐ **C** full-time   ☐ **D** permanent

(b) Which word best describes Karl's job? **(1 mark)**
☐ **A** outside   ☐ **B** exciting   ☐ **C** varied   ☐ **D** stationary

Job interview

Here you can prepare for a Higher role play task in the Speaking exam.

Vorstellungsgespräch

Ich bin höflich und freundlich.
I am polite and friendly.
Ich habe keine Erfahrung, aber ich lerne schnell.
I don't have any experience, but I learn fast.
Ich babysitte / mache Babysitting.   I babysit.
Ich komme gut mit anderen Menschen aus.
I get on well with other people.
Ich arbeite gern in einem Team.
I like working in a team.
Ich habe einen Erste-Hilfe-Kurs besucht.
I have done a first aid course.
Letztes Jahr habe ich zwei Wochen bei einer
  Firma gearbeitet.
Last year I worked at a company for two weeks.
Möchten Sie meinen Lebenslauf sehen?
Would you like to see my CV?

Different words for 'you'

Familiar
du = 'you' to another young person, family member, friend or animal
ihr = 'you' plural of du

Sie du

Formal
Sie = 'you' to adult(s), teacher(s), official(s)
Sie = singular and plural

Questions in a job interview

Wie sind die Arbeitsstunden?
What are the hours?
Gibt es gute Aufstiegsmöglichkeiten?
Are there good promotion prospects?
Wie viel Urlaub werde ich pro Jahr bekommen?
How much holiday will I get each year?

Worked example

 SPEAKING

Instructions to candidate: You are having a telephone interview for a job as a waiter in a Swiss hotel. Your teacher will play the role of the hotel manager and will speak first.

Task
Du möchtest als Kellner/in in der Schweiz arbeiten.
Du hast ein Vorstellungsgespräch am Telefon mit dem Manager / der Managerin.

1 Job
– Guten Tag. Was für einen Job suchen Sie?
– Ich interessiere mich für den Job als Kellner/in in Ihrem Restaurant.

2 Der Job – Gründe
– Warum möchten Sie in einem Restaurant arbeiten?
– Ich habe schon Erfahrung und ich arbeite gern mit Leuten zusammen.

3 !
– Welche Arbeitserfahrung haben Sie schon -
Welche Arbeitserfahrung haben Sie schon gehabt?
– Letztes Jahr habe ich in einem Eiscafé in meiner Stadt gearbeitet.

Exam alert

Get the register right – here, you are talking to a potential employer, i.e. an older person you do not know, so definitely **Sie**.

- See page 9 for role play advice.
- See page 106 for question words.

Grund = one reason, Gründe = reasons. Make sure you give two pieces of information to score full marks.

Role play strategy

Don't try to show off complex language in the role play – your aim is to communicate, so use constructions you are secure with. You can use the other Speaking parts of the exam to impress with more complex language!

Now try this

Listen to the recording

 SPEAKING TRACK 46

Now practise the whole role play yourself, including the final two prompts: Listen to the audio file containing the teacher's part and fill in the pauses with your answers:

4 ? Arbeitsstunden   5 ? Kleidung

Languages beyond the classroom

Collect a good stock of verbs for the Writing and Speaking exams, to add variety to your work.

Sprachen für überall

Traum (m)	dream
Fremdsprache (f)	foreign language
Fremdsprachenassistent/in (m/f)	
foreign language assistant	
Dolmetscher/in (m/f)	interpreter
Übersetzer/in (m/f)	translator
im Ausland leben	to live abroad
Leute kennenlernen	to get to know people
neue Freundschaften aufbauen	
to build new friendships	
um die Welt reisen	to travel the world
sich neue Erlebnisse aussuchen	
to look for new experiences	
in ein neues Land ziehen	
to move to a new country	
an internationalen Konferenzen teilnehmen	
to take part in international conferences	

Verbs

befehlen	to order / command
beschließen	to decide
erlauben	to allow
erreichen	to reach
erwarten	to expect
forschen	to research
helfen	to help
nennen	to call
raten	to advise
reden	to talk
schauen	to look
scheinen	to seem
stecken	to place
vermeiden	to avoid
versprechen	to promise
wechseln	to change
zeigen	to show

Worked example

Arbeiten mit Sprachen

Lies diesen Artikel über Übersetzer und Dolmescherjobs.

> Ohne Fremdsprachen geht es heute weniger denn je – gleich ob auf Reisen, im Studium oder im Beruf. Es gibt also gute Gründe, möglichst früh Fremdsprachen zu lernen und diese Sprachkenntnisse ein Leben lang zu pflegen.
>
> Georg: „Ich habe Portugiesisch und Finnisch in der Schule gelernt, also kann ich auch in diese beiden Sprachen dolmetschen."
>
> Diese Aussage ist leider falsch. Man kann nur in eine Sprache dolmetschen, die man ausgezeichnet beherrscht. Die Zielsprache ist im Idealfall die Muttersprache. Dolmetscher müssen sofort reagieren, Informationen schnell verarbeiten und das Gesagte klar und flüssig – ohne allzu viele Ähs und Ähms – in der anderen Sprache wiedergeben können.

Beantworte die Frage **auf Deutsch**. Vollständige Sätze sind nicht nötig.

(a) Nenne **einen** Grund, warum Fremdsprachen wichtig sind.   **(1 mark)**

sie helfen auf Reisen / beim Lernen/ bei der Arbeit

Answering questions in German

☑ Do **not** just copy extracts from the text as your answer – you will not get a mark for it.

☑ You can repeat individual words, but your answers must be in your own words to gain full marks.

☑ Although vollständige Sätze (complete sentences) are not necessary, you will need to supply your own verbs to answer.

Now try this

Now read the above extract on the left again and complete the reading activity.

(b) Warum kann Georg nicht als Dolmetscher arbeiten?   **(1 mark)**

(c) Was muss man als Dolmetscher vermeiden?   **(1 mark)**

- Answer **in German**.
- Question (a) asks for **one** reason for **one** mark. Other reasons that would also score a mark are: **sie helfen bei der Arbeit / beim Lernen**.

Volunteering

When talking about volunteering experiences, include time expressions with past tense modals: Zuerst musste ich … (First I had to …) or Danach sollte ich … (Afterwards I was supposed to …).

Freiwillig arbeiten

Ich habe …   I …

… freiwillige Arbeit geleistet.
… did voluntary work.

…eine Woche bei einem Wohltätigkeitsverein verbracht.
… spent a week at a charity.

… Aufgaben / Textverarbeitung gemacht.
… did tasks / word-processing.

… Akten abgeheftet.   … did filing.

… viele Anrufe gemacht.
… made lots of phone calls.

… neue Fähigkeiten gelernt.
… learnt new skills.

… eine Spendeaktion organisiert.
… organised a charity event.

Das hat großen Eindruck gemacht.
That made a big impression.

Die Erfahrung war sehr lehrreich.
The experience was very educational.

Adverbs of time

Usually, the verb must come second:
Dann habe ich in der Klinik geholfen.
Then I helped in the clinic.

danach   afterwards   vorher   beforehand
dann   then   zuerst   first of all

With bevor and nachdem, the verb goes to the end:
Nachdem ich mit den Kindern gespielt hatte, war ich erschöpft.
After I'd played with the children, I was exhausted.

Ich habe Geld zu Gunsten einer Kindergruppe gesammelt.
I raised money in aid of a children's group.

Worked example

LISTENING TRACK 47

Hunger an der Tür

You hear a radio interview with Frau Kahn from the charity „Hunger an der Tür". What does she say?

Listen to the recording

(a) Choose the **two** correct answers.

☐ **A** The charity is campaigning against homelessness.

☐ **B** The charity has over a million volunteers.

☒ **C** The charity is campaigning against child poverty.

☐ **D** 1.6 million children don't have a home.

☒ **E** The problem is increasing.

(2 marks)

– Morgen werden wir mit tausenden unserer freiwilligen Helfer zum Reichstag fahren, um gegen die Kinderarmut in Deutschland zu protestieren. Mehr als 1,6 Millionen Kinder leben in einem Haushalt, wo es nicht genug zu essen gibt. Und die Zahl nimmt ständig zu.

Exam alert

Read the answer options and the rubric to get yourself 'in the zone' of the topic. Then listen to the whole passage to get the gist. Do any of the options strike you straight away as being wrong? If so, cross them out with a pencil. On the second listening, double check the audio against the remaining options. Only **two** are correct.

Now try this

LISTENING TRACK 48

Now complete the activity below.

Listen to the recording

(b) Choose the **two** correct answers.

☐ **A** The charity is targeting parents.

☐ **B** The charity is targeting the children directly.

☐ **C** Volunteers are often at risk.

☐ **D** Volunteers buy families new clothes.

☐ **E** Volunteers help parents with job seeking.

(2 marks)

Training

Make sure you can refer to the different locations on a photo so that you can give a precise description in the exam.

Lehrlinge

Arbeitspraktikum (n)	work experience
Ausbildungszentrum (n)	training centre
Betriebspraktikum (n)	work experience
Lehrling (m)	apprentice
Praktikum (n)	internship
in die Berufsschule gehen	to go to vocational college
eine Ausbildung machen	to do training
eine Lehre machen	to do an apprenticeship
Man muss ...	You have to ...
Aufgaben ausführen.	do tasks.
Kaffee kochen.	make coffee.
Akten abheften.	do filing.
Telefonanrufe beantworten.	answer phone calls.
Kunden anrufen.	pbone customers.
abends lernen.	study in the evenings.
einen Kurs besuchen.	do a course.

Man hat viel / wenig / keinen Kontakt mit Kunden.
You have a lot / little / no contact with customers.
Man ist sehr / nicht beschäftigt.
You are very / not busy.

Positions on a photo

When describing a photo, don't forget about your word order:
Man sieht eine Frau links. ➡ Links sieht man eine Frau.

im Hintergrund   oben

links   rechts

unten   im Vordergrund

Describing a photo

☑ Don't worry if you don't know all the words for the items you can see – concentrate on those you **do** know how to say.

☑ German is great for inventing your own words. In the worked example you could use *ein blauer Arbeitsanzug* (work suit) to describe the outfit this apprentice is wearing. Be **creative** with language!

Worked example

SPEAKING

Work

Schau dir das Foto an und sei bereit, über Folgendes zu sprechen:

• Beschreibung des Fotos

Im Vordergrund sieht man ein Mädchen. Ich denke, sie ist ein Lehrling und sie arbeitet heute in einer Werkstatt. Ein älterer Mann erklärt, wie die Maschine funktioniert. Das Mädchen trägt einen blauen Arbeitsanzug, weil die Arbeit manchmal schmutzig ist. Vielleicht muss sie manchmal eine Brille tragen, weil die Arbeit gefährlich für die Augen sein kann.

Have a go at adapting this sample answer for the description part of the task: Beschreibung des Fotos.

Exam alert

The 'picture-based' conversation should be around three minutes in length. This includes all **five** of the teacher's questions. Here, you are only dealing with the first of those five questions, so go for an answer that will be around 30 seconds in length.

Now try this

SPEAKING

Now prepare to talk on the subject of these bullet points as fully as you can:
• deine Meinung zum Arbeitspraktikum
• Erzählung über eine Arbeit, die du gemacht hast
• was du bei einem Arbeitspraktikum machen willst
• deine Meinung, ob eine Ausbildung machen oder studieren besser ist.
Try to speak for at least 30 seconds on each point.

Record yourself and play it back to see if you hesitated!

Part-time jobs

When talking about part-time jobs, always use a range of vocabulary and structures, including weil, bevor and obwohl.

Der Teilzeitjob

Ich arbeite samstags als ...	I work on Saturdays as a ...
Kassierer/in	cashier
Kellner/in	waiter / waitress
Tellerwäscher/in	washer-upper
Verkäufer/in	sales assistant

Ich trage Zeitungen aus.
I deliver newspapers.

Ich habe einen Ferienjob in einem Restaurant.
I've got a holiday job in a restaurant.

Ich habe einen Teilzeitjob in einer Autowerkstatt.
I've got a part-time job at a garage.

Ich verdiene 10 Euro pro Stunde.
I earn 10 euros an hour.

Mein Ziel ist es, einen Sommerjob zu finden.
It's my aim to find a summer job.

Ich bin ein erfahrener Babysitter / eine erfahrene Babysitterin.
I am an experienced babysitter.

Ich hefte gern Sachen ab.   I enjoy filing.

This / that, these / those, every, which

Grammar page 88

These follow the pattern of der, die, das (see page 85).

dieser	this / these
jener	that / those
jeder	every
welcher?	which?

	nom	acc	dat
masc	dieser	diesen	diesem
fem	diese	diese	dieser
neut	dieses	dieses	diesem
plural	diese	diese	diesen

(m acc) Welchen Job würdest du lieber machen?
Which job would you prefer to do?

(f acc) Ich finde jede Arbeit ermüdend.
I find every job tiring.

(n dat) Ich möchte in diesem Restaurant arbeiten.
I would like to work in this restaurant.

Worked example

Ein Teilzeitjob

Beschreibe deinen Teilzeitjob.

> Jeden Samstag arbeite ich von neun bis dreizehn Uhr im Tanzstudio. Ich helfe beim Unterricht und verdiene dafür sechs Euro pro Stunde. Der Job gefällt mir sehr, weil Tanzen mein Lieblingshobby ist.

Aiming higher

> In den Sommerferien habe ich als Kellner in einer sehr beliebten Bar im Stadtzentrum gearbeitet. Am Anfang war ich sehr nervös, weil ich vorher noch nie in einem Restaurant gearbeitet hatte. Zwar war es sehr anstrengend, den Gästen den ganzen Tag die Getränke und Mahlzeiten zu servieren, aber es hat auch riesigen Spaß gemacht, besonders wenn die Gäste sympathisch waren.

Remember to include opinions.

Exam alert

Make sure you include some of these points in a piece of writing to help achieve a higher grade:

- excellent linking of the piece into a whole
- coherent and pleasant to read
- well-manipulated language which produces longer and more fluent sentences.

This uses lots of exciting structures: imperfect, pluperfect, **zwar** + inversion, both positive and negative opinions.

Now try this

Describe your (real or imaginary) part-time job, in about 100 words.

CV

You may want to include some details about yourself from your CV in the Speaking and Writing exams.

Mein Lebenslauf

persönliche Daten (pl)	personal details
Geburtsdatum (n) und -ort (m)	date and place of birth
Schulbildung (f)	education
Berufsausbildung (f)	training
Arbeitserfahrung (f)	work experience
Zukunftsträume (pl)	future dreams
Sonstiges	other

Etwas, nichts, wenig + adjective

Try to include some of these higher-level phrases, which convert an adjective into a noun.

viel Interessantes	a lot of interesting things
etwas Spannendes	something exciting
wenig Gutes	not much / little good
nichts Besonderes	nothing special

Worked example

Ein Bewerbungsbrief

Dein Manager als zukünftige/r Fremdsprachenassistent/in möchte einiges über dich wissen.

Schreibe eine Antwort an ihn.

Du **musst** diese Punkte einschließen:
• Beschreibung deiner Schulbildung
• ob du Arbeitserfahrung hast
• wo du jetzt arbeitest
• deine Zukunftsträume für die Arbeit.

Schreibe ungefähr 80–90 Wörter **auf Deutsch**.

Aiming higher

Ich bin am 11. August 1999 in Bath geboren.
Ich war fünf Jahre lang in der St.-Thomas-Schule und ich habe in zehn Fächern gute Noten bekommen.
Für das Arbeitspraktikum habe ich eine Stelle in einem Gartenbetrieb gefunden. Ich interessiere mich sehr für Pflanzen und arbeite am liebsten im Freien.
Sonnabends bin ich immer im Hallenbad zu finden, wo ich kleinen Kindern das Schwimmen beibringe. Ich finde das toll, weil ich gut mit jungen Leuten auskomme. Ich würde sagen, dass ich freundlich, geduldig, sportlich und ziemlich selbstbewusst bin. Ich bin aber auch ehrgeizig und möchte eines Tages eine erfolgreiche Karriere machen.

Writing strategies

The best answers use structures that show your level of knowledge and application.

✗ **Don't** overcomplicate your work – stick to structures you are familiar with and get them (and the word order) right.

✗ **Don't** overuse the same verbs: ist / war, hat / hatte and es gibt /gab are great, but don't use them all the time.

✗ Regard long lists as verboten (banned!) because a top answer will **never** include long lists of nouns. Here, the student mentions good grades in ten subjects, and leaves it at that.

✓ Make sure you include a good variety of grammatical structures and idioms – make every word count.

Now try this

Now write 80–90 words about the bullet points to complete the activity.

Ich bin am ... in ... geboren.
Meine Lieblingsfächer sind ..., weil ...
Ich habe Erfahrung als ... Ich habe ...
In den Sommerferien habe / bin ich ...
Nächstes Jahr werde ich ...

Global sports events

World sports events touch everyone these days, so make sure you are prepared to talk about them.

Sportveranstaltungen

Besucher (m)	visitor
Eintrittskarte (f)	entry ticket
Fernsehkanal (m)	television channel
Gastfreundschaft (f)	hospitality
Meisterschaft (f)	championship
Nationalmannschaft (f)	national team
Olympische Spiele (pl)	Olympic Games
Publikum (n)	audience
Schiedsrichter (m)	referee
Sportausrüstung (f)	sports equipment
Stadion (n)	stadium
Turnier (n)	tournament
Zuschauer (m)	spectator

In meiner Stadt haben sie ein enormes Stadion gebaut.
They have built a huge stadium in my town.
Hier fehlt es an Sportevents.
There is a lack of sports events here.
Kein Einwohner hat von der Meisterschaft profitiert.
No inhabitant has benefited from the championship.

Using als

Use als to mean 'when' in the **past** tense. It sends the verb to the end of the clause, then there is a **comma** before the next verb.

Als ich jünger war, habe ich die Olympischen Spiele in London besucht.
When I was younger I went to the Olympic Games in London.

Als er für die Nationalmannschaft gespielt hat, hat er viele Tore geschossen. When he played for the national team, he scored lots of goals.

Worked example

Sport
Übersetze **ins Deutsche**.

> Countries across the world can benefit from sports events. When I went to the Olympic Games in Brazil it was a wonderful experience.

Länder überall auf der Welt können von Sportveranstaltungen profitieren. Als ich zu den Olympischen Spielen in Brasilien gefahren bin, war das ein wunderbares Erlebnis.

Making the translation suit you

It is unlikely that you will know **every** word or phrase in any given translation, so you need to work on strategies to adapt words to the knowledge you **do** have. Here are some examples:

Forgotten ...		Why not use ... ?
plural of 'country'	➡	jedes Land (every country)
'across'	➡	in or auf
'world'	➡	Planet (m)
'events'	➡	Spiele, Feste, Wettbewerbe

Now try this

Now complete the translation **into German**.

> Although Brazil is a poor country, they had built a wonderful stadium for athletics and lots of people had bought tickets. The aim of a sportsman or a sportswoman is certainly to win a medal at a championship.

- 'had built' = pluperfect tense!
- 'aim' could also be 'wish' or 'desire'.

Global music events

Music festivals and concerts are shared around the world, thanks to the internet. Have you ever been to or watched one yourself?

Musikfeste

Eintrittsgeld (n)	entry fee
Kleidung (f)	clothes
Musiker/in (m/f)	musician
Prominente (m/f)	celebrity
Tanzen (n)	dancing
Welt (f)	world
Werbung (f)	advert
Zelt (n)	tent
ermüdend	tiring
unglaublich	unbelievable
unvorstellbar	unimaginable
zusammen	together

24-hour clock

The 24-hour clock is easy if you know your numbers. It is used for opening times, train times or to say when an event is taking place.

 neun Uhr dreißig

 zwölf Uhr fünfundvierzig

 sechzehn Uhr fünfzehn

 zwanzig Uhr vierzig

 dreiundzwanzig Uhr

Das Musikfest war ein unvergessliches Erlebnis. The music festival was an unforgettable experience.

Worked example

Instructions to candidate:
You are buying tickets for an international music festival. Your teacher will play the role of the ticket seller and will speak first.

Task
Du telefonierst mit der Musikorganisation. Du willst Eintrittskarten kaufen.

1 Eintrittskarte
– Was möchten Sie kaufen?
– Zwei Eintrittskarten für ein Konzert.

2 Tag und Uhrzeit
– Wann ist das Konzert?
– Es ist am Dienstag um halb neun.

3 !
– Warum wollen Sie es sehen?
– Ich liebe die Band.
– Prima.

Exam alert

You have to use **your initiative** in these role play situations – as long as your questions and statements are relevant to the situation, they will be OK. Play to your own strengths and use language you are comfortable with.

See also page 9 for more on role plays.

Number of tickets + event is enough to cover the two details needed here.

This student knows the time expression: **am** + day / date and **um** + time.

This response answers the unexpected question – more is not needed.

Now try this

   TRACK 49

Now practise the whole role play yourself, including the final two prompts. Listen to the audio file containing the teacher's part and fill in the pauses with your answers:

4 Transport – was und Grund
5 ? Preis

 Listen carefully to the recording to help improve your pronunciation.

 Listen to the recording

Being green

Make sure you can say what you do and do **not** do in respect of the environment.

Grünes Leben

Energie sparen	to save energy
weniger Strom / Gas benutzen	to use less electricity / gas
Wasser nicht verschwenden	not to waste water
Lichter ausschalten	to turn off lights
Fenster und Türen zumachen	to close windows and doors
sich wärmer anziehen	to dress more warmly
die richtige Mülltonne benutzen	to use the correct rubbish bin
den Müll trennen	to separate the rubbish
Dosen / Flaschen recyceln	to recycle cans / bottles
Speisereste kompostieren	to compost leftover food
mit dem Rad fahren	to go by bike
mit den öffentlichen Verkehrsmitteln fahren	to travel by public transport
eine Fahrradwoche organisieren	to organise a cycling week
an einer Umweltaktion teilnehmen	to take part in an environmental campaign

Negatives

If you want to say what you do **not** do to help the environment, use kein (not a / none) or nicht (not) with a verb.

Unser Haus hat keine Solarenergie.
Our house has no solar energy.
Er recycelt nicht gern.
He does **not** like recycling.

Listening tips

- The listening passages are not very long, so concentrate hard on **every word** to find the answers.
- If you do not understand every word, try to pick up on key words, cognates and parts of words, which may lead you to the answer.

Worked example

LISTENING TRACK 50

Umweltaktion
You hear a report about the environment. What does it say?

(a) Listen to the recording and put a cross ✗ in the correct box.

Example: This report is about …

Listen to the recording

- ☐ **A** traffic
- ☐ **B** energy
- ☒ **C** living creatures
- ☐ **D** recycling

— Letztes Jahr haben wir an unserer Schule keine Aktion für Menschen gemacht. Stattdessen haben wir uns auf die Natur konzentriert und daher auf dem Schulhof Nistkästen für Vögel entworfen.

Watch out for **kein** here! This campaign had nothing to do with people!

Now try this

LISTENING TRACK 51

Now complete the listening activity by putting a cross ✗ in the correct box for each of these reports.

(b) This report is about …

Listen to the recording

- ☐ **A** traffic
- ☐ **B** recycling
- ☐ **C** acting responsibly
- ☐ **D** walking to school

(c) This report is about …

- ☐ **A** eating healthily
- ☐ **B** growing vegetables
- ☐ **C** acting responsibly
- ☐ **D** rubbish

(d) This report is about …

- ☐ **A** reducing food bills
- ☐ **B** energy
- ☐ **C** endangered animals
- ☐ **D** second-hand clothes

Protecting the environment

Having a good selection of idioms will help you across the topics, so learn a few from this page to have up your sleeve!

Umweltschutz

globale Erwärmung (f)	global warming
Klimawandel (m) / Klimawechsel (m)	climate change
Pflanze (f)	plant
Regenwald (m)	rainforest
Schutz (m)	protection
Tierart (f)	animal species
Tiere (pl)	animals
Verschmutzung (f)	pollution
retten	to save
schützen	to protect
umweltbewusst	environmentally aware
umweltfeindlich	environmentally damaging
umweltfreundlich	environmentally friendly

Idioms

Viel Glück!	Good luck!
Es ist mir egal.	I don't mind / care.
Meiner Meinung nach ...	In my opinion ...
Es kommt darauf an.	It depends.
Es macht nichts.	It doesn't matter.
Es lohnt sich (nicht).	It is (not) worth it.
Das ist in Ordnung.	That is OK.
Das ist schade.	That is a shame.
Genug davon.	Enough of that.

Hals- und Beinbruch!
Break a leg!

Worked example

50 einfache Dinge, die man tun kann, um die Welt zu retten **by Andreas Schlumberger**

Lies diesen Text über den Klimawandel.

Mit Energie gegen den Klimakollaps

Der Klimawechsel – da sind sich die Experten einig – kommt, ja ist schon im Gange. Wir stehen nicht mehr vor der Aufgabe, ihn zu vermeiden, sondern vielmehr, seinen Effekt zu begrenzen und Strategien zu entwickeln, um uns daran anzupassen.

Jeder weiß, dass der Mensch einen großen Anteil an der Klimaerwärmung hat und dass die Folgen sich negativ auf die Menschheit auswirken werden. Für Mitteleuropa sind extreme Wetterereignisse wie Stürme oder Starkregen und auch extremes Wetter wie zum Beispiel Dürren oder Überschwemmungen zu erwarten. Hitzewellen werden zur Norm. Besonders stark könnten auch die Alpenregionen unter dem Klimawandel leiden.

Beantworte die Frage **auf Deutsch**. Vollständige Sätze sind nicht nötig.

(a) Wer glaubt fest an den Klimawechsel?

(1 mark)

jeder Experte / alle Experten

Prepositions

Make sure less common prepositions don't catch you out! Here are some you may come across:

außer + dative	except for
bei + dative	at, at the home of
gegen + accusative	against
ohne + accusative	without
trotz + genitive	in spite of
wegen + genitive	because of

Now try this

Now read the extract again and complete the reading activity.

gelingen is a dative verb meaning 'to succeed'.

(b) Was ist uns nicht gelungen? **(1 mark)**

(c) Was ist das Einzige, was wir dagegen machen können? **(1 mark)**

(d) Warum sind wir daran schuld? **(1 mark)**

(e) Was wird die größte Auswirkung des Klimawandels sein? **(1 mark)**

(f) Welches Gebiet wird besonders unter dem Klimawandel leiden? **(1 mark)**

Natural resources

When discussing or writing about certain topics, it is extremely useful to use the man form to express what people do generally.

Naturschätze

Kohle (f)   Gas (n)   Öl (n)   Tiere (pl)

Salzwasser (n)   Pflanzen (pl)   Erde (f)

Bauer (m) / Bäuerin (f)	farmer
Meer (n)	ocean
Obst und Gemüse (n)	fruit and vegetables
Umwelt (f)	environment
drohen	to threaten
retten	to save
vergiften / kontaminieren	to poison

Der Bauer muss immer auf die Natur auf seinen Feldern aufpassen.
The farmer always has to look after nature in his fields.

Der Klimawandel bedroht unsere Inseln und Meere.
Climate change threatens our islands and oceans.

Man sollte immer Obst und Gemüse aus der Gegend kaufen.
You should always buy fruit and vegetables from the area.

Wir müssen unsere Umwelt retten.
We have to save our environment.

Using man

- Man is used in German much more than 'one / you' is used in English.
- Use man to mean 'one / you / they / we / somebody / people'.
- Man takes the er / sie part of the verb (man hat).

Present tense

Man hilft bei Problemen.
They help with problems.

Past tense

Man hat einen Brief geschrieben.
Somebody wrote a letter.

Future tense

Man wird das verbessern.
We will improve that.

Don't confuse man with der Mann (the man).

Worked example

Umweltorganisation

Du arbeitest für eine Umweltorganisation in Österreich. Eine Schule sucht Informationen über umweltfreundliches Leben.

Schreibe eine formelle Antwort mit diesen Informationen:
- wie man umweltfreundlich einkauft
- wie man unterwegs Energie spart
- wie man die Umwelt schützen kann
- eine Umweltaktion für nächstes Jahr.

Schreibe ungefähr 40–50 Wörter **auf Deutsch.**   (16 marks)

Sehr geehrte Frau Bach,
am besten kaufen Sie immer frisches Gemüse auf dem Markt ein. Fahren Sie mit öffentlichen Verkehrsmitteln oder dem Rad, um Energie zu sparen. Wenn Sie zu Hause sind, machen Sie die Fenster und Türen zu, um weniger Strom zu benutzen. Nächstes Jahr können Sie eine Umweltaktion organisieren, um Pflanzenarten zu schützen.

- This is a short formal writing task – you only need to write about ten words for each bullet point, so don't go over the top with your response. Concentrate on writing simple, accurate sentences in German – capital letters for nouns, words spelled accurately and punctuation where required.
- If you are addressing somebody such as Frau Bach, you must use the formal Sie register throughout. Slang and du forms have no place here.

Now try this

Now complete the writing activity for yourself.

Campaigns

You may well come across a reading or a listening passage about campaigns across the globe. Make sure you know these key words and phrases, so you are prepared.

Aktionen

Armut (f)	poverty
Krieg (m)	war
Mangel (m)	lack of
Menschen / Leute (pl)	people
Menschenrechte (pl)	human rights
Sicherheit (f)	security
Umweltorganisation (f)	environmental organisation
helfen	to help
bedürftig	needy
unglücklich	unfortunate
fairer Handel (m)	fair trade
freiwillig arbeiten	to work voluntarily

Um ... zu ...

Grammar page 94

Place a comma before um ... zu + infinitive verb to convey 'in order to' do something.

Ich sammele Geld, um Kindern in Afrika zu helfen.

I am collecting money (in order) to help children in Africa.

Ich mache Poster, um Leute auf das Problem aufmerksam zu machen.

I am making posters (in order) to make people aware of the problem.

In English you don't always need to say 'in order to', but just 'to'.

Worked example

 LISTENING TRACK 52

Global campaigns

You hear a radio report about the organisation 'Kind International'.

What does it say?

Listen to the recording and put a cross ✗ in the correct box.

Listen to the recording

Example: ☒ The charity has been going for ten years.

☐ **A** 'Kind International' campaigns to provide education.

☐ **B** The charity only supports girls.

☐ **C** Boys choose to go and fight.

☐ **D** The charity raises money for Europe.

☐ **E** The charity raises awareness in Europe.

Reading options carefully

✓ Don't miss small words in the answer options, such as 'only'. This is key to getting the answer correct, so don't misread statement **B** as 'The charity supports girls.' 'Only' is the word you need!

✓ Similarly, the prepositions 'for' and 'in' in statements **D** and **E** are crucial.

— Bei „Kind International"
kämpfen wir seit zehn Jahren für
Menschenrechte in aller Welt.

Now try this

 LISTENING TRACK 53

Now listen to the rest of the recording and choose the **two** correct answers from above. **(2 marks)**

Listen to the recording

- **als** can mean 'as' (as well as 'when' in the past)!
- **je mehr ... desto** + comparative = the more ... the ...

Good causes

Practise the sounds of the alphabet when you are working to improve your German pronunciation.

Wohltätigkeitsverein

Dürre (f)	drought
Erdbeben (n)	earthquake
Hungersnot (f)	famine
Orkan (m)	hurricane
Trinkwasser (n)	drinking water
Überschwemmung (f)	flood
Unglück (n)	catastrophe
Vulkan (m)	volcano
leiden (an)	to suffer (from)
sterben	to die
überleben	to survive
Briefe schreiben	to write letters
Geld sammeln	to raise money
Leuten helfen	to help people
Menschen unterstützen	to support people

The alphabet

Try to speak German words clearly and with a good accent. Use the listening passages from this book to help practise pronunciation.

Listen to the recording

A ah	**B** beh	**C** tseh	**D** deh	**E** eh	**F** eff
G geh	**H** hah	**I** ee	**J** yot	**K** kah	**L** ell
M emm	**N** enn	**O** oh	**P** peh	**Q** kuh	**R** err
S ess	**T** teh	**U** oo	**V** fow	**W** veh	**X** iks
Y upsilon	**Z** tsett	**Ä** ah umlaut	**Ö** oh umlaut	**ü** uh umlaut	**ß** ess-tsett

Make sure you are familiar with the German alphabet, so that if a word is spelled out you know the letters.

Worked example

Globale Probleme

Du teilst dieses Foto online mit deinen Freunden.

Beschreibe das Foto **und** schreibe deine Meinung über globale Probleme.

Schreibe ungefähr 20–30 Wörter **auf Deutsch**.

(12 marks)

Das Bild zeigt eine Katastrophe und viele Leute sind im Freien und wohnen in Zelten. Meiner Meinung nach sind diese Probleme schrecklich, weil so viele Kinder leiden.

Use **diese** instead of **die** to emphasise 'these' problems when writing or talking about a photo.

You can adapt descriptions such as these to use in more detailed writing or speaking tasks on this topic.

Short writing task

- The task asks you to describe the photo **and** give an opinion. You **must** do both.
- Do not repeat language – always think of a different way of expressing something to avoid repetition.
- Accuracy is key here – check your work at the end for spellings, capital letters and sense!

Now try this

Now write 20–30 words **in German** for your answer to the photo task.

Gender and plurals

When you are learning a German noun, always learn it with its word for 'the' (gender).
All German words are masculine, feminine or neuter.

Der, die, das (the)

Every German noun is masculine (m – der),
feminine (f – die) or neuter (n – das).
Der Mann ist groß.
The man is tall.
Die Frau ist klug.
The woman is clever.
Das Kind ist nervig.
The child is annoying.
Die Katzen sind süß.
The cats are cute.

	masc	fem	neut	pl
nominative	der	die	das	die

If you don't know the gender of a word, you
can look it up in a dictionary.

Frau *f* woman, wife

Der, die, das as the subject

The definite articles der, die, das, die are used
when the noun is the **subject** of the sentence.
That means it is doing the action of the verb.
Der Lehrer spielt Fußball.
The teacher is playing football.
This is called the **nominative** case.

Look at pages 86–87 for more
details of the cases in German.

Der, die, das as the object

But if the teacher becomes the **object** of the
verb, e.g. is seen by someone else, then **der**
changes to **den**.
Ich sehe den Lehrer.   I see the teacher.
I = subject, as it is doing the seeing, and the
teacher is the object, as he is being seen.
This is called the **accusative** case – die and das
stay the same when used in this way.

	masc	fem	neut	pl
accusative	den	die	das	die

Plurals

German nouns have different plurals. Not
sure what they are? Check in a dictionary.

The part in brackets tells you what to add to
make the word plural. The umlaut before the -er
ending tells you that an umlaut is added to the
vowel before the ending, so the plural of **Mann**
is Männer.

Mann (¨er) *m* man

Now try this

Which definite article – **der**, **die** or **das**? Use a
dictionary to find the gender and plural of these nouns.
(a) Anmeldung   (d) Haltestelle
(b) Fahrer   (e) Fernseher
(c) Rührei   (f) Brötchen

The gender is taken from the last
word of compound nouns: **der Abend**
+ **das Brot** = **das Abendbrot**.

Cases and prepositions

Prepositions such as durch (through) and zu (to) trigger a change in der, die or das, as they have to be followed by a specific case – the accusative, dative or genitive.

Changes to 'the'

	masc	fem	neut	pl
nominative	der	die	das	die
accusative	den	die	das	die
dative	dem	der	dem	den
genitive	des	der	des	der

Changes to 'a'

	masc	fem	neut	pl
nominative	ein	eine	ein	keine
accusative	einen	eine	ein	keine
dative	einem	einer	einem	keinen
genitive	eines	einer	eines	keiner

The genitive is not used very often, but it looks impressive if you can use it correctly!

keine – not a / no

Prepositions + accusative

Prepositions that trigger a change to the **accusative** case:

für	for
um	around
durch	through
gegen	against / towards
entlang	along (after the noun)
bis	until
ohne	without

FUDGEBO = first letters of all accusative prepositions!

Ich kaufe ein Geschenk für einen Freund.
I am buying a present for a friend.

Geh um die Ecke.
Go round the corner.

Prepositions + dative

Prepositions that trigger a change to the **dative** case:

aus	from	nach	after
außer	except	seit	since
bei	at, at the home of	von	from
gegenüber	opposite	zu	to
mit	with		

nach einer Weile — after a while
Fahr mit dem Bus. — Go by bus.

zu + dem = zum
zu + der = zur
bei + dem = beim

You need to add -n to the end of a plural masculine or neuter noun in the dative case:
mit meinen Freunden = with my friends.

Prepositions + genitive

Prepositions that trigger a change to the **genitive** case:

trotz	in spite of / despite
wegen	because of

See page 70 for more prepositions + genitive.

laut der Zeitung	according to the newspaper
wegen des Wetters	because of the weather
während	during

You also need to add an -s to the end of a masculine or neuter noun in the genitive case.

Now try this

Translate these phrases **into German** by adding the preposition and changing the word for 'the' or 'a'.

(a) against the wall (*die Mauer*)
(b) except one child (*ein Kind*)
(c) despite the snow (*der Schnee*)
(d) after an hour (*eine Stunde*)
(e) to the shops (*die Geschäfte – pl*)
(f) without a word (*ein Wort*)
(g) during the summer (*der Sommer*)
(h) at the doctor's (*der Arzt*)

Dative and accusative prepositions

Movement towards or not? That is the key question! Dual-case prepositions can be followed by either the accusative or the dative case.

Dual-case prepositions

an	at
auf	on
hinter	behind
in	in
neben	next to
über	over
unter	under
vor	in front of
zwischen	between

- If there is **movement towards** a place, these prepositions trigger a change to the **accusative** case.
  Ich gehe ins Haus. = I go into the house.

- If there is **no movement** towards a place, these prepositions trigger a change to the **dative** case.
  Ich bin im Haus. = I am in the house.

  in + das = ins
  in + dem = im

Verbs + accusative

Some verbs work with a preposition followed by the accusative case.

aufpassen auf	to look after
sich ärgern über	to be annoyed about
sich gewöhnen an	to get used to
sich streiten über	to argue about
sich erinnern an	to remember
sich freuen auf	to look forward to
warten auf	to wait for

Ich muss auf den Hund aufpassen.
I have to look after the dog.
Ich freue mich auf den Sommer.
I am looking forward to the summer.
Ich habe mich an die Arbeit gewöhnt.
I have got used to the work.

Prepositional phrases

Die Katze springt auf den Tisch. (acc)	The cat jumps onto the table.
Die Katze sitzt auf dem Tisch. (dat)	The cat is sitting on the table.
Ich surfe gern im Internet. (dat)	I like surfing the net.
Sie wohnt auf dem Land. (dat)	She lives in the countryside.
auf der linken Seite (dat)	on the left-hand side

As you can see here, where there is no movement the dual-case preposition is generally followed by the dative case, and where there is a sense of movement it is followed by the accusative.

Now try this

Complete the sentences with the correct definite article ('the').

(a) Ich wohne an .... Küste (f).

(b) Sie streiten sich über .... Fernseher (m).

(c) Was gibt es hinter .... Haus (n)?

(d) Wie finden Sie die Geschichte über .... Jungen (pl)?

(e) Die Nacht vor .... Hochzeit (f).

(f) Man muss zwischen ....Zeilen (pl) lesen.

(g) Denke an .... Namen (m).

(h) Erinnerst du dich an .... Person (f)?

Dieser / jeder, kein / mein

Other groups of words, such as adjectives, also change according to case.

Words that follow the der, die, das pattern

These words follow the pattern of der, die, das:

dieser (this)   jeder (each)   jener (that)
mancher (some)   solcher (such)   welcher (which)

dieser Mann   this man
bei jeder Gelegenheit   at every opportunity
jedes Mal   every time

	masc	fem	neut	pl
nominative	dieser	diese	dieses	diese
accusative	diesen	diese	dieses	diese
dative	diesem	dieser	diesem	diesen

Ways to use these words

dieses und jenes	this and that
in dieser Hinsicht	in this respect
jeder Einzelne	every individual
jeder Zweite	every other
zu jener Zeit / Stunde	at that time / hour
mancher Besucher	many a visitor / some visitors
Mit solchen Leuten will ich nichts zu tun haben.	I don't want to have anything to do with such people.
Welche Größe haben Sie?	What size are you?

Words that follow the ein pattern

These words follow the pattern of ein:

kein (not a)

mein (my)   unser (our)
dein (your)   euer (your, plural)
sein (his)   Ihr (your, polite)
ihr (her)   ihr (their)

	masc	fem	neut	pl
nominative	kein	keine	kein	keine
accusative	keinen	keine	kein	keine
dative	keinem	keiner	keinem	keinen

Ways to use these words

keine Ahnung	no idea
mein Fehler	my mistake
gib dein Bestes	do your best
sein ganzes Leben	his whole life
ihr Ziel ist es ...	it's her / their aim ...
als unser Vertreter	as our representative
auf euren Handys	on your mobiles
Ihr Zeichen	your reference
für ihre Schularbeit	for her / their schoolwork

ich habe keine Lust – I don't want to + infinitive with zu

meiner Meinung nach (dat) – in my opinion

Now try this

Translate the sentences **into English**.
(a) Ich habe keine Lust, einkaufen zu gehen.
(b) Sie hat ihr ganzes Taschengeld für Kleidung ausgegeben.
(c) Solche Leute werden schnell unhöflich.
(d) Ich finde mein Leben langweilig.
(e) Dieses Mal fahren wir mit dem Zug.
(f) Seine Eltern sind arbeitslos.
(g) Solche Regeln finde ich dumm.
(h) Welches Buch liest du?

Adjective endings

Refer to the tables on this page to check you are using adjective endings correctly in your exam preparation work.

Adjective endings with the definite article 'the'

You can also use these endings after dieser (this), jener (that), jeder (each), mancher (some), solcher (such) and welcher (which). The endings are either -e or -en!

	masc	fem	neut	pl
nominative	der kleine Hund	die kleine Maus	das kleine Haus	die kleinen Kinder
accusative	den kleinen Hund	die kleine Maus	das kleine Haus	die kleinen Kinder
dative	dem kleinen Hund	der kleinen Maus	dem kleinen Haus	den kleinen Kindern

Siehst du den kleinen Hund? Can you see the little dog?

Adjective endings with the indefinite article 'a'

You can also use these endings after kein (not a), mein (my), dein (your), sein (his), ihr (her / their), unser (our), euer (your, pl) and Ihr (your, polite).

	masc	fem	neut	pl
nominative	ein kleiner Hund	eine kleine Maus	ein kleines Haus	meine kleinen Kinder
accusative	einen kleinen Hund	eine kleine Maus	ein kleines Haus	meine kleinen Kinder
dative	einem kleinen Hund	einer kleinen Maus	einem kleinen Haus	meinen kleinen Kindern

Ich wohne in einem kleinen Haus. I live in a little house.

Adjective endings with no article

	masc	fem	neut	pl
nominative	kleiner Hund	kleine Maus	kleines Haus	kleine Kinder
accusative	kleinen Hund	kleine Maus	kleines Haus	kleine Kinder
dative	kleinem Hund	kleiner Maus	kleinem Haus	kleinen Kindern

Kleine Kinder sind oft süß. Little children are often cute.

Many of these are similar to the definite articles: das Haus – kleines Haus, der Mann – großer Mann.

Now try this

Complete the sentences using the adjectives in brackets with their correct endings.

(a) Ich habe .... Noten in Deutsch. (ausgezeichnet) (pl)

(b) Im Jugendklub kann ich .... Essen kaufen. (warm) (n)

(c) Ich suche ein .... Bett. (preisgünstig) (n)

(d) Die .... Lage war sehr praktisch. (zentral) (f)

(e) Spanien ist ein .... Urlaubsziel der Deutschen. (beliebt) (n)

(f) Das ist eines der .... Lieder des Jahres. (meistverkauft) (pl)

(g) Letztes Wochenende gab es einen .... Sonntag. (verkaufsoffen) (m)

(h) Stell keine .... Daten ins Netz. (persönlich) (pl)

Had a look ☐ Nearly there ☐ Nailed it! ☐

Comparisons

To aim high, you will need to use comparatives and superlatives, so always think of a way to include them in your speaking and writing work.

Formation

Add -er for the comparative, as in English (loud ➡ louder).

Add -(e)ste for the superlative 'most'.

Ich bin laut.   I am loud.

Ich bin lauter als du.
I am louder than you.

Ich bin die lauteste Person.
I am the loudest person.

- Adjectives are the same as adverbs, so you can compare how somebody does something very easily.

Ich schreie laut.   I shout loudly.

Ich schreie lauter   I shout more loudly
  als du.   than you.

Ich schreie am   I shout the loudest.
  lautesten.

- Comparative and superlative adjectives have to agree with the noun they are describing.

die schöneren   the prettier earrings
  Ohrringe

der lustigste Junge   the funniest boy

Irregular comparatives

Some adjectives have small changes in the comparative and superlative forms.

alt ➡	älter ➡	älteste
old	older	oldest
jung ➡	jünger ➡	jüngste
young	younger	youngest
groß ➡	größer ➡	größte
big	bigger	biggest
gut ➡	besser ➡	beste
good	better	best
lang ➡	länger ➡	längste
long	longer	longest
hoch ➡	höher ➡	höchste
high	higher	highest

Gern, lieber, am liebsten

Use gern (like), lieber (prefer) and am liebsten (like most of all) to compare your likes and dislikes.

gern and lieber go after the verb:
Ich spiele gern Schach.
I like playing chess.
Ich schwimme lieber.
I prefer swimming.
Use am liebsten to start your sentence:
Am liebsten fahre ich Ski.
Most of all I like skiing.

Lieblingssport (m) – favourite sport
Lieblingsgruppe (f) – favourite group

Now try this

Complete the sentences with a comparative or superlative form.

(a) Mathe ist viel .... als Chemie. (einfach)

(b) Mein Bruder ist.. als meine Schwester. (jung)

(c) Dieses Lied ist doch.. als der letzte Schlager. (gut)

(d) Meiner Meinung nach ist Physik .... als Chemie. (nützlich)

(e) Ich habe das .... Zimmer im Haus. (winzig)

(f) Das .... Fach in der Schule ist Informatik. (langweilig)

(g) Meine Stadt ist das.. Urlaubsziel in Deutschland. (beliebt)

(h) Letztes Jahr hatte ich die .... Noten in der Klasse. (schlecht)

Look at page 89 to check your endings.

Personal pronouns

Just like der, die and das, pronouns change depending on which case they are in – the nominative, accusative or dative case.

Pronouns

Pronouns = he, him, their, her, she, etc.

nominative	accusative	dative
ich	mich	mir
du	dich	dir
er / sie / es	ihn / sie / es	ihm / ihr / ihm
wir	uns	uns
ihr	euch	euch
Sie / sie	Sie / sie	Ihnen / ihnen

- Use pronouns to avoid repeating nouns:
  Ich mag Dieter, weil er nett ist.
  I like Dieter because he is nice.
- When a noun is the **accusative object** of the sentence, you need to use the **accusative pronoun**:
  Ich sehe ihn.   I see him.
- Use the correct pronoun after a preposition, depending on whether the preposition takes the accusative or dative case:
  bei mir (dat)   at my house
  für ihn (acc)   for him

Dative pronoun phrases

These expressions need a dative pronoun:

Es tut mir leid.	I am sorry.	Wie geht's dir / Ihnen?	How are you?
Es gefällt ihm.	He likes it.	Es geht uns gut.	We are well.
Es fällt mir schwer.	I find it difficult.	Es gelingt mir.	I succeed.
Es tut ihr weh.	It hurts her.	Es hilft ihnen.	It helps them.
Das schmeckt mir.	That tastes good / I like the taste.	Es scheint ihnen, dass ...	It seems to them that ...
Sport macht ihr Spaß.	She finds sport fun.	Das ist uns egal.	We don't mind about that.

Sie or du?

Familiar

du = 'you' to another young person, family member / friend, animal
ihr = 'you' plural of du (more than one young person, etc.)

Formal

Sie = 'you' to adult(s), teacher(s), official(s)
Sie = singular and plural

Sie   du

Now try this

Choose the correct pronoun to complete each sentence.
(a) Nina ist sympathisch, obwohl .... manchmal auch launisch ist.
(b) Es tut .... leid, aber ich kann nicht zur Party kommen.
(c) Seit wann geht es .... schlecht, Leon?
(d) Wir sind ins Theater gegangen, aber leider hat ....das Stück nicht gefallen.
(e) Mein Freund geht .... auf die Nerven, aber ich will nicht mit .... Schluss machen.
(f) Hast du Zeit, ... bei den Hausaufgaben zu helfen?

Word order

German word order follows rules – learn the rules and your sentences will be in the correct order.

Verb in second place

The **verb** never comes first – it is always in second place!

1 **2** **3**   **1** **2** **3**

Ich   fahre   mit dem Auto.   Jeden Tag   fahre ich   mit dem Auto.

Perfect tense

Form of haben / sein goes in second position:

1 **2** **3** **4**

Gestern   bin ich   mit dem Auto   gefahren.

Future tense

Form of werden goes in second position:

1 **2** **3** **4**

Morgen   werde ich   mit dem Auto   fahren.

Modals

Form of modal goes in second position:

1 **2** **3** **4**

Ich   will   mit dem Auto   fahren.

Remember:
ich werde – I will / I am going to
ich will – I want to

Time – Manner – Place

A detail of transport counts as Manner, so put it **after** a Time expression, but **before** a Place.

T gestern / heute / letzte Woche / in Zukunft

M mit dem Zug / zu Fuß / mit meiner Familie

P nach London / in die Stadt / über die Brücke

T   **M**   **P**

Ich fahre heute   mit dem Zug   nach Bonn.
Today I am going   by train   to Bonn.

Linking words

No word order change here!

| aber | but | oder | or |
| denn | because | und | and |

Ich spiele gern Tennis und ich fahre gern Rad.
I like playing tennis and I like cycling.
Ich esse gern Pommes, aber ich esse nicht gern Bratkartoffeln.
I like eating chips but I don't like roast potatoes.

Now try this

Order the sentences following the above rules.

(a) fahre / ich / ins Ausland / gern
(b) Verkehrsamt / findet / Informationen / beim / man
(c) gesund / ich / normalerweise / esse
(d) sehen / manchmal / Filme / wir / im Jugendklub
(e) arbeiten / ich / im Sportzentrum / möchte / im Juli
(f) habe / gearbeitet / ich / in einem Büro / letztes Jahr
(g) gehen / ins Kino / werde / mit meiner Mutter / morgen / ich

 Try to invert your sentences by starting with a time expression rather than **ich, du,** etc.

Conjunctions

You will be expected to use plenty of conjunctions, such as weil, wenn and als, in your speaking and writing work – and you will **have** to show that you can use them correctly.

Verb to the end

Weil (because) sends the verb ➡ to the **end** of the clause.

Ich rede über Adele, weil sie meine Lieblingssängerin ist.
I am talking about Adele because she is my favourite singer.

Ich gehe nicht gern ins Kino, weil das zu teuer ist.
I don't like going to the cinema because it is too expensive.

All these conjunctions send the verb to the end of the clause, just like weil:

als	when (one occasion, past tense)	nachdem	after
		ob	whether
		obwohl	although
bevor	before	während	while
bis	until	was	what
da	because / since	wie	how
		wenn	when / if (present or future)
damit	so that		
dass	that		
		wo	where

Perfect tense

- In the **perfect** tense, the form of haben / sein is **last** in a clause.

  Ich kann nicht zur Party kommen, obwohl ich meine Hausaufgaben gemacht habe.
  I can't come to the party although I have done my homework.

- Watch out for the **verb, comma, verb** structure.

  Als ich klein war, habe ich viel im Garten gespielt.
  When I was small I played in the garden a lot.

Form of **haben** / **sein** in the perfect tense ➡ right to the end.

Future tense and modals

- In the **future** tense, it is the form of werden which goes last.

  Da ich nach Afrika reisen werde, muss ich zum Arzt.
  Because I am going to travel to Africa, I have to go to the doctor.

- With **modal** verbs, it is the modal itself which is last in the clause.

  Ich bin immer glücklich, wenn ich ins Konzert gehen darf.
  I am always happy when I am allowed to go to the concert.

Form of **werden** ➡ right to the end.
Form of modal ➡ right to the end.

Now try this

Join each pair of sentences using the subordinating conjunction in brackets.
(a) Ich habe bei meiner Großmutter gewohnt. Meine Mutter war im Krankenhaus. (während)
(b) Ich bin ins Café gegangen. Ich habe ein T-Shirt gekauft. (nachdem)
(c) Ich war in Spanien im Urlaub. Ich habe einen neuen Freund kennengelernt. (als)
(d) Er ist sehr beliebt. Er ist nicht sehr freundlich. (obwohl)
(e) Ich werde für eine neue Gitarre sparen. Ich finde einen Nebenjob. (wenn)
(f) Ich bin froh. Ich habe gute Noten in der Schule bekommen. (dass)
(g) Ich muss meine Eltern fragen. Ich darf ins Konzert gehen. (ob)
(h) Er hat mir gesagt. Er will mit mir ins Kino gehen. (dass)

More on word order

There are a few more structures here that you should try to fit into your work to improve your writing and speaking. They also affect word order, so be careful!

Using um ... zu ...

Um ... zu ... means 'in order to' and is used in German where English might just say 'to'. It requires an infinitive verb at the end of the clause.

Ich trage Zeitungen aus,
  um Geld zu verdienen.

infinitive verb

I deliver newspapers, (in order) to earn money.

- Only use um ... zu ... where you would say 'in order to' in English, even if you drop the 'in order' bit.
- The verb after um ... zu ... is always in the infinitive and at the **end**.
- Add a comma before um.

ohne ... zu ... means without. It works in the same way:
Ich bin in die Schule gegangen, ohne ihn zu sehen. I went to school without seeing him.

Infinitive expressions

These expressions with zu need an infinitive.

ich ... (I ...)	hoffe, ... (hope)	+ zu + infinitive
	versuche, ... (try)	
	beginne / fange an, ... (begin)	
	habe vor, ... (intend)	
	nutze die Chance, ... (use the opportunity)	

Ich hoffe, Deutsch zu studieren.
I hope to study German.

Ich versuche, einen guten Job zu bekommen.
I am trying to get a good job.

With separable verbs, zu goes after the prefix.
Ich habe vor, fernzusehen.   I intend to watch TV.

Relative pronouns

Relative pronouns send the verb to the end of the clause.

They are used to express **who** or **that** or **which**.

m Der Mann, der im Café sitzt, ist Millionär.
The man who is sitting in the café is a millionaire.

f Die Katze, die unter dem Tisch schläft, ist sehr süß.
The cat that is sleeping under the table is very sweet.

n Das Mädchen, das einen roten Rock trägt, singt in einer Band.
The girl who's wearing a red skirt sings in a band.

Now try this

1 Combine the sentences with **um ... zu ...** .
   (a) Ich fahre nach Italien. Ich besuche meine Verwandten.
   (b) Ich gehe zum Sportzentrum. Ich nehme 5 Kilo ab.
2 Combine the clauses with **zu**.
   (a) Ich versuche – ich helfe anderen.
   (b) Ich habe vor – ich gehe auf die Uni.
3 Combine the sentences with a relative pronoun.
   (a) Das ist das Geschäft. Das Geschäft verkauft tolle Kleidung.
   (b) Hier ist eine Kellnerin. Die Kellnerin ist sehr unhöflich.

The present tense

There are regular and irregular present tense verbs for you here, but look at page 100 for the super-irregular verbs haben (to have) and sein (to be).

Present tense regular

Verbs change according to who is doing the action, just like in English: I drink ➡ he drinks.

The present tense describes what is happening now and can be translated as 'drink' or 'am drinking'.

machen – to do / to make		
ich	mache	I do / make
du	machst	you do / make
er / sie / es	macht	he / she / it does / makes
wir	machen	we do / make
ihr	macht	you do / make
Sie / sie	machen	you / they do / make

infinitive verb

wir / Sie / sie forms = same as infinitive

- The present tense is used to describe what you are **doing now** or what you **do** regularly.
- Present tense time expressions include:

  jetzt (now)   heute (today)
  im Moment   (at the moment)
  dienstags   (on Tuesdays)

- You can use the present tense with a time phrase to indicate the **future**:

  Morgen fahre ich nach London.
  Tomorrow I am going to London.

Present tense vowel changes

Some verbs have a vowel change in the du and er / sie / es forms of the present tense, but they still have the same endings (-e, -st, -t, etc.).

geben – to give			
ich	gebe	wir	geben
du	gibst	ihr	gebt
er / sie /es	gibt	Sie / sie	geben

infinitive verb

vowel change

nehmen – to take	
ich	nehme
du	nimmst
er / sie / es	nimmt

essen – to eat	
ich	esse
du	isst
er / sie / es	isst

schlafen – to sleep	
ich	schlafe
du	schläfst
er / sie / es	schläft

Sie schläft.

Now try this

Complete the sentences with the correct form of the present tense verb in brackets.

(a) Ich .... gern Musik. (hören)

(b) Meine Schwester .... in ihrem eigenen Zimmer. (schlafen)

(c) Ihr .... montags schwimmen, oder? (gehen)

(d) .... du gern Wurst mit Senf? (essen)

(e) Wir .... nie mit dem Auto. (fahren)

(f) Was .... Sie in den Sommerferien? (machen)

(g) .... es eine Ermäßigung für Senioren? (geben)

(h) Mein Bruder .... heute im Bett, weil er krank ist. (bleiben)

Separable and reflexive verbs

To aim for a higher grade, include separable and reflexive verbs in your speaking and writing work.

Separable verbs

These verbs have two parts: a prefix +
the main verb. They go their separate
ways when used in a sentence.

Ich sehe oft fern.   I often watch TV.
Ich mache immer die Türen zu.
I always close the doors.

aufwachen	to wake up
aussteigen	to get off
einsteigen	to get on
fernsehen	to watch TV
herunterladen	to download
hochladen	to upload
umsteigen	to change (trains, trams, buses)
zumachen	to close

Make sure you can use separable
verbs in all the tenses.

Present: Ich steige in Ulm um.
             I change in Ulm.
Perfect: Ich bin in Ulm umgestiegen.
             I changed in Ulm.

> Separable verbs form the past participle
> as one word with **-ge-** sandwiched
> in the middle: **zugemacht** (closed),
> **ferngesehen** (watched TV).

Future: Ich werde in Ulm umsteigen.
            I will change in Ulm.
Modals: Ich muss in Ulm umsteigen.
            I have to change in Ulm.

Reflexive verbs

Reflexive verbs need a reflexive pronoun – mich,
dich, etc.

sich freuen – to be happy / pleased	
ich freue mich	wir freuen uns
du freust dich	ihr freut euch
er / sie / es freut sich	Sie / sie freuen sich

• Note that **sich** never has a capital letter.
• **sich freuen auf ...** (acc) – to look forward
  to ...

sich amüsieren	to enjoy oneself
sich befinden	to be located
sich entscheiden	to decide
sich erinnern an	to remember
sich langweilen	to be bored
sich interessieren für	to be interested in

Ich interessiere mich für Geschichte.
I am interested in history.

All reflexive verbs use **haben** in the perfect
tense.
Er hat sich angezogen.   He dressed.
Wir haben uns gelangweilt.   We were bored.

Now try this

1 Translate the sentences **into German**.
   (a) I watch TV. I watched TV.
   (b) I change trains at six o'clock. I changed
       trains at six o'clock.
   (c) I download music. I will download music.
   (d) I got on. I have to get on.

2 Complete the sentences with the correct
   reflexive pronoun.
   (a) Ich erinnere .... kaum an meinen
       Vater.
   (b) Wir interessieren .... für Mode.
   (c) Habt ihr .... im Jugendklub
       gelangweilt?
   (d) Meine Schule befindet .... am
       Stadtrand.

Commands

Use this page to help you give commands and orders accurately.

Sie commands

Swap the present tense round so that the verb comes before the pronoun:

Sie hören (you listen) ➡ Hören Sie! Listen!

Schreiben Sie das auf Deutsch auf.
Write that down in German.

Gehen Sie hier links.   Go left here.

- Separable verbs separate and the prefix goes to the end of the sentence.
  Tauschen Sie nicht Ihre Telefonnummer aus.
  Don't swap your phone number.
- Sein (to be) is irregular.
  Seien Sie nicht aggressiv.
  Don't be aggressive.

Du commands

Use the present tense du form of the verb minus the -st ending:

gehen ➡ du gehst ➡ du gehst ➡ Geh!

Bleib anonym.   Stay anonymous.

Triff niemanden allein.
Don't meet anyone on your own.

Beleidige andere nicht.
Don't insult others.

Such dir einen Spitznamen aus.
Choose a nickname.

This is a separable verb so it splits.

Some verbs are irregular in the present tense, so make sure you get them right when giving commands.

haben – to have	➡	Hab (Spaß)! – Have (fun)!
sein – to be	➡	Sei (ruhig)! – Be (quiet)!
essen – to eat	➡	Iss! – Eat!
fahren – to drive	➡	Fahr! – Drive!
geben – to give	➡	Gib das her! – Give me that!
lassen – to leave	➡	Lass! – Leave!
nehmen – to take	➡	Nimm! – Take!

Other Sie commands

Gas weg!	Reduce your speed!
Gefahr!	Danger!
Warnung!	Warning!
Achtung!	Attention! / Watch out!
Vorsicht!	Be careful!
Verboten!	Forbidden!
Kein Eintritt! ⊖	Keep off! / Keep out!
Nicht betreten!	No entry!
Ausfahrt freihalten!	Keep exit clear!
⚠ Lebensgefahr!	Danger of death!
Privatgrundstück	Private land

Now try this

What is this sign asking dog owners to do?

Liebe Hundehalter, bitte achten Sie auf Ihre Lieblinge und benutzen Sie Grünflächen und Wege nicht als Hundetoilette.

Vielen Dank!

Present tense modals

Modal verbs need another verb in the infinitive form, e.g. gehen (to go), kaufen (to buy).
The modal verb comes second in the sentence, while the infinitive is shifted to the very end.

Können (to be able to)

ich / er / sie / es	kann
du	kannst
ihr	könnt
wir / Sie / sie	können

Ich kann nicht schwimmen.   I can't swim.

Müssen (to have to / must)

ich / er / sie / es	muss
du	musst
ihr	müsst
wir / Sie / sie	müssen

Du musst deine Hausaufgaben machen.
You have to do your homework.

Wollen (to want to)

ich / er / sie / es	will
du	willst
ihr	wollt
wir / Sie / sie	wollen

Er will nicht umsteigen.
He doesn't want to change (trains).

Dürfen (to be allowed to)

ich / er / sie / es	darf
du	darfst
ihr	dürft
wir / Sie / sie	dürfen

Wir dürfen in die Disko gehen.
We are allowed to go to the disco.

Sollen (to be supposed to)

ich / er / sie / es	soll
du	sollst
ihr	sollt
wir / Sie / sie	sollen

Germans most often use the imperfect
tense of sollen to express the sense of
'should' or 'ought'.

Ich sollte meine Großeltern besuchen.
I should visit my grandparents.

Mögen (to like)

The present tense of mögen no longer
tends to be used in the present tense
with another verb to express liking.
Instead, the subjunctive form is far more
likely to be used in the sense of 'would
like to'.

ich / er / sie / es	möchte
du	möchtest
ihr	möchtet
wir / Sie / sie	möchten

Sie möchte Rollschuhlaufen gehen.
She would like to go rollerblading.
Ich möchte nicht ins Kino gehen.
I would not like to go to the cinema.

Now try this

Write modal sentences using the verbs given in brackets.
(a) Ich gehe um einundzwanzig Uhr ins Bett. (müssen)
(b) In der Schule raucht man nicht. (dürfen)
(c) Du sparst Energie. (sollen)
(d) Hilfst du mir zu Hause? (können)
(e) Ich fahre in den Ferien Ski. (wollen)
(f) Ich sehe nicht fern. (mögen)
(g) Ich löse das Problem nicht. (können)

 Note that separable verbs come
together as infinitives: ich sehe
fern = fernsehen.

Imperfect modals

Using modals and an infinitive in different tenses is a great way to incorporate a variety of tenses into your work.

Imperfect modals

Infinitive: können – to be able to

Present tense:
ich kann + infinitive at end – I can …

Imperfect tense:
ich konnte + infinitive at end – I was able to …

Ich konnte nicht mehr warten.
I couldn't wait any more.

infinitive at the end

The endings change, depending on the subject of the verb.

ich	konnte
du	konntest
er / sie / es / man	konnte
wir	konnten
ihr	konntet
Sie / sie	konnten

Other modals in the imperfect

* These modals work in the same way as konnte – just add the correct ending.
* There are no umlauts on imperfect tense modals.

müssen	➡ musste	had to
wollen	➡ wollte	wanted to
dürfen	➡ durfte	was allowed to
sollen	➡ sollte	was supposed to
mögen	➡ mochte	liked

Was musstet ihr gestern in Mathe machen?
What did you have to do in maths yesterday?
Er wollte doch nur helfen.
He only wanted to help.
Sie durfte ihn nicht heiraten.
She wasn't allowed to marry him.
Du solltest eine Tablette nehmen.
You should take a pill.

Subjunctive modals (Higher)

Add an umlaut to konnte and mochte and you have the subjunctive. This allows you to talk about things you **could / would** do.

imperfect	➡	subjunctive
konnte	➡	könnte (could) + infinitive
mochte	➡	möchte (would like)

The subjunctive has the same structure as imperfect modals with the infinitive at the end.

Möchtest du ins Kino gehen?
Would you like to go to the cinema?
Das Schwimmbad könnte geschlossen sein.
The swimming pool could be closed.

Now try this

1 Rewrite these sentences with an imperfect tense modal.
  (a) Ich mache Hausaufgaben. (müssen)
  (b) Sie helfen mir nicht. (können)
  (c) Er kauft eine neue Hose. (wollen)
  (d) Wir laden die Fotos hoch. (sollen)
  (e) In der Schule kaut man nie Kaugummi. (dürfen)
  (f) Alle Schüler bleiben bis sechzehn Uhr. (müssen)

2 Rewrite these with a subjunctive modal.
  (a) Es wird schwierig. (können)
  (b) Ich tausche die gelbe Jacke um. (mögen)

The perfect tense 1

The perfect tense is the tense most used to talk about the past in German – using it is a necessity at any level of your GCSE.

The perfect tense

- Use the perfect tense to talk about something you have done in the **past**.
- The perfect tense is made up of **two parts**:

  the correct form of **haben** or **sein** + past participle at the end.

  Ich habe Musik gehört. I listened to music.

Past participles generally start with ge-.

spielen ➡ gespielt (played)

lachen ➡ gelacht (laughed)

fahren ➡ gefahren (drove)

Hast du den Film gesehen?
Have you seen the film?

The perfect tense – haben

Most verbs use haben (to have) in the perfect tense:

form of haben + sentence + past participle at the end.

ich habe	
du hast	gekauft (bought)
er / sie / es hat	gemacht (made)
wir haben	besucht (visited)
ihr habt	gesehen (saw)
Sie / sie haben	

Er hat im Reisebüro gearbeitet.
He worked at the travel agency.
Wir haben Frühstück gegessen.
We ate breakfast.

The perfect tense – sein

Some verbs of movement use sein (to be) to make the perfect tense:

form of sein + sentence + past participle at the end.

ich bin	
du bist	gegangen (went)
er / sie / es ist	geflogen (flew)
wir sind	gefahren (drove / went)
ihr seid	geblieben (stayed)
Sie / sie sind	

Sie ist zu Fuß gegangen.
She went on foot.
Ich bin nach Freiburg gefahren.
I went to Freiburg.

There are some verbs that use **sein** in the perfect tense where there is no apparent movement: **bleiben** (to stay) is an example.

Now try this

Write these sentences in the perfect tense.
- **(a)** Ich kaufe eine Jacke.
- **(b)** Wir fliegen nach Portugal.
- **(c)** Ich sehe meinen Freund.
- **(d)** Lena und Hannah gehen in die Stadt.
- **(e)** Ich besuche meine Tante.
- **(f)** Ich bleibe im Hotel.
- **(g)** Was isst du zu Mittag?
- **(h)** Am Samstag hört er Musik.

Put the form of **haben** / **sein** in **second** position and the past participle at the end of the sentence.

The perfect tense 2

Spotting past participles will help you to identify when a text is in the past tense – but watch out for the hidden ge- in separable verbs such as ferngesehen (watched TV).

Regular past participles

- Begin with ge-.
- End in -t.

Remove -en from the infinitive and replace with -t: machen ➡ macht ➡ gemacht
Das hat ihr Spaß gemacht.
That was fun for her.

Some exceptions

Verbs starting with be-, emp- or ver- do not add ge- to form the past participle.

Ich habe ...	I ...
besucht	visited
empfohlen	recommended
vergessen	forgot
verloren	lost

Separable verbs add **ge-** between the prefix and the main verb:
hochgeladen – uploaded   heruntergeladen – downloaded

Irregular past participles

There are no rules for forming irregular past participles – but here are some common ones to learn.

Ich	gegessen	ate
habe ...	getrunken	drank
	genommen	took
	geschlafen	slept
	geschrieben	wrote
	gesungen	sang
	getragen	wore / carried
	getroffen	met
	gestanden	stood
Ich bin ...	gerannt	ran
	geschwommen	swam
	gewesen	have been
	gestiegen	climbed
	gestorben	died
	geworden	became

Word order

The past participle goes at the **end** of the sentence and the form of haben or sein is in **second** position:

Er   ist   ins Kino   gegangen.
He went to the cinema.

Am Montag   habe ich Fußball   gespielt.
I played football on Monday.

When the verb has already been sent to the end by a conjunction such as weil (because) or als (when), the part of haben or sein comes **after** the past participle:

Ich war dankbar, weil er mein Portemonnaie gefunden hat.
I was grateful because he found my purse.
Als er angekommen war, war er erschöpft.
When he arrived, he was exhausted.

Now try this

Complete the sentences with the correct past participle of the verb in brackets.

(a) Ich habe zu viele Kekse .... (essen)

(b) Haben Sie gut .... ? (schlafen)

(c) Wir haben uns am Bahnhof .... (treffen)

(d) Ich war krank, weil ich den ganzen Tag .... habe. (stehen)

(e) Ich weiß, dass du .... bist. (umsteigen)

(f) Warum hast du die E-Mail .... ? (schreiben)

(g) Ich habe ihr .... , dass sie nicht mitkommen sollte. (empfehlen)

(h) Ich war traurig, als er .... ist. (sterben)

The imperfect tense

If you are telling a story about the past or recounting a series of events in the past, use the imperfect tense.

Forming the imperfect tense

- Take the infinitive, e.g. hören (to hear).
- Take off the final -en ➡ hören = hör.
- Add these endings:

ich hörte	I heard / was hearing
du hörtest	you heard / were hearing
er / sie / es / man hörte	he / she / it / one heard / was hearing
wir hörten	we heard / were hearing
ihr hörtet	you heard / were hearing
Sie / sie hörten	you / they heard / were hearing

Ich hörte gar nichts.   I didn't hear a thing.

Sie spielten drei Jahre lang in der Gruppe.
They played for three years with the group.

Don't forget to use the imperfect modals – see page 99 for a reminder.

'To have' and 'to be' in the imperfect

haben

ich hatte	I had
du hattest	you had
er / sie / es / man hatte	he / she / it / one had
wir hatten	we had
ihr hattet	you had
Sie / sie hatten	you / they had

Ich hatte Glück.   I was lucky.

sein

ich war	I was
du warst	you were
er / sie / es / man war	he / she / it / one was
wir waren	we were
ihr wart	you were
Sie / sie waren	you / they were

Es war teuer.   It was expensive.

Irregular verbs

- Some verbs have irregular stems in the imperfect tense.
- Add the same basic endings as above to the irregular stems on the right:

  ich ging – wir gingen (I went – we went)
  ich fuhr – wir fuhren (I drove – we drove)

Im Stück ging es um eine Beziehung.
The play was about a relationship.
Die Kinder sahen blass aus.
The children looked pale.
Es fand in Hamburg statt.
It took place in Hamburg.

gehen ➡	ging	went
fahren ➡	fuhr	drove
finden ➡	fand	found
kommen ➡	kam	came
nehmen ➡	nahm	took
sehen ➡	sah	saw
sitzen ➡	saß	sat
stehen ➡	stand	stood
tut weh ➡	tat weh	hurt

Es gab is an impersonal verb and so does not change:

Es gab ein Haus.   There was a house.
Es gab zwei Häuser.   There were two houses.

Now try this

Put these sentences into the imperfect tense.
(a) Sie hat Angst.
(b) Es ist hoffnungslos.
(c) Es gibt Toiletten im Erdgeschoss.
(d) Hörst du das?
(e) Plötzlich kommt uns der Mann entgegen.
(f) Das ist eine Überraschung, nicht?
(g) Es ist niemand zu Hause.
(h) Sie spielen gern Tischtennis.

Spielen is a regular verb like hören.

The future tense

As well as using the future tense, you can also express future intent using the present tense. Use this page to check you can do both!

The future tense

Use the future tense to talk about things you **will** do or things that **will** happen in the future:

form of werden (to become) + sentence + infinitive at the end.

ich werde	
du wirst	holen (collect)
er / sie / es / man wird	klopfen (knock)
wir werden	mieten (rent)
ihr werdet	zelten (camp)
Sie / sie werden	

Word order in the future tense

Form of werden in second position:

Nächste Woche werde ich in Urlaub fahren.

Ich werde erfolgreich sein.
I will be successful.
Wie groß wirst du werden?
How tall will you get?
Morgen wird es kalt sein.
It will be cold tomorrow.
Werden sie auf die Uni gehen?
Will they go to university?
Ich bin froh, dass du zu Besuch kommen wirst.
I am happy that you will come to visit.

Reflexive and separable verbs

- Reflexive verbs – add the pronoun after part of werden:
  Ich werde mich schnell rasieren.
  I will shave quickly.

- Separable verbs – stay together at the end of the sentence:
  Er wird das Lied herunterladen.
  He will download the song.

Present tense with future intent

You can use the present tense to express what you are **going to** do. Include a time marker to make it clear that the intent is based in the future.

morgen	tomorrow
übermorgen	the day after tomorrow
nächste Woche	next week

Nächsten Sommer fahren wir nach Amerika.
We are going to America next summer.

Now try this

Rewrite the sentences in the future tense with **werden**.

(a) Ich gewinne das Spiel.
(b) Wir gehen in den Freizeitpark.
(c) Sie mieten eine große Wohnung.
(d) Ihr habt große Schwierigkeiten.
(e) Er besteht die Prüfung.
(f) Nächste Woche ziehen wir um.
(g) Trefft ihr euch später?
(h) Ich ziehe mich um sechs Uhr an.

The conditional

The conditional is very similar in structure to the future tense and using it will improve your writing and speaking.

Conditional

Use the conditional to talk about things you **would** do or things that **would** happen in the future:
part of würde (would) + sentence + infinitive at the end.

ich würde	
du würdest	
er / sie / es / man würde	+ infinitive
wir würden	
ihr würdet	
Sie / sie würden	

Ich würde gern nach Italien fahren.
I would like to go to Italy.
Würden Sie lieber Geschäftsmann oder Klempner werden?
Would you rather become a businessman or a plumber?
Würdest du je rauchen?
Would you ever smoke?
Man würde nie ein Auto kaufen.
We would never buy a car.

würde sein = wäre – would be
würde haben = hätte – would have
es würde geben = es gäbe – there would be

Using wenn

- You often use wenn (if) with the conditional.
- Remember: verb, comma, verb!

Wenn ich reich wäre, würde ich keine Designerkleidung kaufen.
If I were rich, I wouldn't buy designer clothes.

Wenn sie ein Vorstellungsgespräch hätte, würde sie rechtzeitig ankommen.
If she had an interview, she would arrive on time.

Making requests

Use the conditional to make a request for something you **would** like:
Ich möchte Pommes essen.
I would like to eat chips.

The plural form adds -n:
wir möchten   we would like
sie hätten gern   they would like to have

Sie hätte gern ein neues Handy.
She would like a new mobile.

Now try this

Rewrite these sentences using the conditional.
(a) Ich gehe gern ins Theater.
(b) Er kommt nie spät an.
(c) Wir trinken nie Bier.
(d) Helfen Sie mir bitte?
(e) Zum Geburtstag bekommt sie am liebsten Geld.
(f) Nächstes Jahr heiraten sie vielleicht.
(g) Wenn Latein Pflicht ist, gehe ich auf eine andere Schule.
(h) Wenn ich das mache, gibt es Krach mit meinen Eltern.

The pluperfect tense

The pluperfect tense is used to say you **had** done something. Use it to aim for a top grade!

Forming the pluperfect

- Use the pluperfect tense to talk about events which **had** happened.
- It is made from the **imperfect** of haben or sein + past participle.

ich hatte du hattest er / sie / es / man hatte wir hatten ihr hattet Sie / sie hatten	Pause gemacht (had had a break) Freunde gesehen (had seen friends)

ich war du warst er / sie / es / man war wir waren ihr wart Sie / sie waren	Ski gefahren (had been skiing) zu Hause geblieben (had stayed at home)

Haben or sein?

- Some participles take haben and some sein. The rules are the same as for the perfect tense.
  Sie hatte kein Wort gesagt.
  She had not said a word.

ich hatte (I had)	angefangen / begonnen (begun) gearbeitet (worked) gebracht (brought) eingeladen (invited) erreicht (reached) geholt (fetched) gelogen (lied)

Er war nicht gekommen.   He had not come.

ich war (I had)	geblieben (stayed) hineingegangen (entered) eingeschlafen (fallen asleep) vorbeigegangen (gone by)
es war	geschehen (it had happened)

The pluperfect and perfect tenses

Look how similar the pluperfect tense is to the perfect tense.

Ich habe Basketball gespielt. I played basketball.	➡	Ich hatte Basketball gespielt. I had played basketball.
Es hat ihm Spaß gemacht. It was fun for him.	➡	Es hatte ihm Spaß gemacht. It had been fun for him.
Wir sind zur Eishalle gegangen. We went to the ice rink.	➡	Wir waren zur Eishalle gegangen. We had gone to the ice rink.

Now try this

Write these sentences in the pluperfect tense.

(a) Ich habe zu Mittag gegessen.

(b) Sie haben als Stadtführer gearbeitet.

(c) Bist du schwimmen gegangen?

(d) Wir sind in Kontakt geblieben.

(e) Sie sind mit dem Rad in die Stadt gefahren.

(f) Ich habe sie vor einigen Monaten besucht, aber damals war sie schon krank.

(g) Bevor ich ins Haus gegangen bin, habe ich ein Gesicht am Fenster gesehen.

(h) Obwohl ich kaum mit ihm gesprochen habe, schien er sehr freundlich zu sein.

Questions

In the role play task, you will **have** to ask at least one question, so make sure you can do just that by studying this page carefully!

Asking questions

You can swap the pronoun and verb round to form a question:

Du hast einen Hund. You have got a dog.

Hast du einen Hund? Have you got a dog?

Make sure you use a variety of tenses when you ask questions about events at different times:

Sie sind nach Spanien geflogen.

You flew to Spain.

Sind Sie nach Spanien geflogen?

Did you fly to Spain?

Key question words

Wann?	When?
Warum?	Why?
Was?	What?
Wer?	Who?
Wie?	How?
Wo(hin)?	Where (to)?

Wohin werden Sie in Urlaub fahren?

Where will you go on holiday?

Wann sind Sie dorthin gefahren?

When did you go there?

Warum hat Ihnen der Film nicht gefallen?

Why didn't you like the film?

Other question words

Was für ...?	What sort of ...?
Was für Bücher lesen Sie gern?	What sort of books do you like reading?
Wie viele?	How many?
Wie viele Stunden pro Woche treiben Sie Sport?	
How many hours a week do you do sport?	
Wessen?	Whose?
Wessen Idee war das?	Whose idea was that?

Wessen never changes case.

Welchen is in the accusative case.

Using welcher (which)

Welcher agrees with the noun it is asking about.

masc	Welcher Sport? Which sport?
fem	Welche Aufgabe? Which activity?
neut	Welches Fach? Which subject?
pl	Welche Fächer? Which subjects?

Welchen Sport finden Sie am einfachsten?

Which sport do you find the easiest?

Welches Fach machst du am liebsten?

Which subject do you like doing best?

Wen? Wem?	Who(m)?
Wen finden Sie besser?	Who do you find better?
Mit wem spielen Sie Squash?	
Who do you play squash with?	

Wen is in the accusative case.

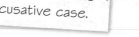

Wem is in the dative case after mit.

Now try this

1 Turn the sentences into questions.
   (a) Sie lesen gern Science-Fiction-Bücher.
   (b) Sie finden Ihre Arbeit anstrengend.
   (c) Sie möchten nur teilzeit arbeiten.
   (d) Nächsten Sommer werden Sie nach Australien auswandern.

2 Write questions **in German** to ask in your role play.
   (a) Who could help me?
   (b) When does the restaurant open?
   (c) Why is there a bag here?
   (d) How can I get to the cathedral?
   (e) What can one do in the evenings?

Time markers

Here are some ideas to introduce a variety of time expressions into your work – remember to put the verb in **second** position if you are starting with one of these.

Present tense

aktuell	current(ly)
heute	today
heutzutage	these days
jetzt	now
seit	since / for

Jetzt, wo ich noch Schülerin bin, muss ich viel lernen.
Now, while I am still a pupil, I must work hard.

Past tenses

gestern	yesterday
vorgestern	the day before yesterday
vor drei Monaten	three months ago
letzte Woche	last week
letztes Wochenende	last weekend
früher	previously
als (kleines) Kind	as a (small) child
neulich	recently

Vor sechs Wochen habe ich mir das Bein gebrochen.
I broke my leg six weeks ago.

Future tense

bald	soon
in Zukunft	in future / in the future
morgen (früh)	tomorrow (morning)
übermorgen	the day after tomorrow
nächste Woche	next week
am nächsten Tag	on the next day

In Zukunft werde ich eine gute Stelle finden.
In the future, I will find a good job.

General

jeden Tag / täglich	every day / daily
wöchentlich	weekly
eines Tages	one day
immer	always
immer noch	still
schon immer	always
am Anfang	at the start
von Zeit zu Zeit	from time to time
sofort	immediately
rechtzeitig	on time
regelmäßig	regularly

Ich habe schon immer in Wales gewohnt.
I have always lived in Wales.

Now try this

Rewrite these sentences with the time expressions provided in brackets.

(a) Ich spiele Klavier. (*for three years*)
(b) Er hat die Hausaufgaben nicht gemacht. (*last week*)
(c) Wir werden in den Bergen wandern gehen. (*next summer*)
(d) Wir wollten das Betriebspraktikum nicht machen. (*at the start*)
(e) Man wird alle Lebensmittel elektronisch kaufen. (*in future*)
(f) Ich hoffe, Disneyland zu besuchen. (*one day*)
(g) Ich hatte Halsschmerzen. (*the day before yesterday*)
(h) Sie spielen oft Tennis. (*earlier*)

 Watch the tense!

Numbers

Numbers are really important in a variety of contexts so make sure you know them!

Numbers

1 eins	11 elf	21 einundzwanzig	100 hundert
2 zwei	12 zwölf	22 zweiundzwanzig	101 hunderteins
3 drei	13 dreizehn		200 zweihundert
4 vier	14 vierzehn		333 dreihundertdreiunddreißig
5 fünf	15 fünfzehn		
6 sechs	16 sechzehn		
7 sieben	17 siebzehn	30 dreißig	
8 acht	18 achtzehn	40 vierzig	
9 neun	19 neunzehn	50 fünfzig	1000 tausend
10 zehn	20 zwanzig	60 sechzig	
		70 siebzig	ein Tausend a thousand
		80 achtzig	eine Million a million
		90 neunzig	eine Milliarde a billion
			eine Billion a trillion

all one word – however long!

no und after hundert

Ordinal numbers

1ˢᵗ erste	11ᵗʰ elfte	am vierzehnten März	on 14 March
2ⁿᵈ zweite	12ᵗʰ zwölfte	ab dem achten Juni	from 8 June
3ʳᵈ dritte	13ᵗʰ dreizehnte	vom ersten bis zum	from 1 to 13
4ᵗʰ vierte	14ᵗʰ vierzehnte	dreizehnten Dezember	December
5ᵗʰ fünfte		nach / vor dem zehnten April	after / before
6ᵗʰ sechste	20ᵗʰ zwanzigste		10 April
7ᵗʰ siebte	21ˢᵗ einundzwanzigste	seit dem dritten Februar	since 3 February
8ᵗʰ achte	30ᵗʰ dreißigste	**Years**	
9ᵗʰ neunte	31ˢᵗ einunddreißigste	(im Jahr)	
10ᵗʰ zehnte		neunzehnhundertachtundachtzig	in 1988
		(im Jahr)	
		zweitausendzwanzig	in 2020

Now try this

 LISTENING TRACK 55

 Listen to the recording

Listen and fill in the numbers.

(a) ☐ . – ☐ . Mai   **(d)** ☐ . Januar ☐   **(g)** ☐

(b) ☐   **(e)** € ☐ Millionen   **(h)** ☐ Grad

(c) € ☐ , ☐   **(f)** ☐ % Ermäßigung

Vocabulary

These pages cover key German vocabulary that you need to know. This section starts with general terms that are useful in a wide variety of situations and then divides into vocabulary for each of the five main topics covered in this revision guide:

1 High frequency language   **2** Identity and culture   **3** Local area, holidays and travel

4 School   **5** Future aspirations, study and work   **6** International and global dimension

F Sections to be learnt by **all** candidates   **H** Sections to be learnt by **Higher** candidates only

Learning vocabulary is essential preparation for your Reading and Listening exams. Don't try to learn too much at once – concentrate on learning and testing yourself on a page at a time.

1 High frequency language

Verbs A–E		Verbs E–K		Verbs L–S	
abfahren	to depart	enden	to finish, end	lächeln	to smile
anfangen	to begin	erklären	to explain	lachen	to laugh
ankommen	to arrive	erlauben	to allow	lassen	to leave
annehmen	to accept	erreichen	to reach	laufen	to walk, run
anrufen	to phone	erzählen	to tell	leben	to live
antworten	to answer	fallen	to fall	legen	to lay
arbeiten	to work	fallen lassen	to drop	leihen	to borrow, hire
aufhören	to stop	fehlen	to miss	lesen	to read
aufmachen	to open	fernsehen	to watch TV	lieben	to love
ausgeben	to spend	finden	to find	liegen	to lie
ausleihen	to lend	fliehen	to escape	lügen	to tell a lie
bedienen	to serve	folgen	to follow	meinen	to think, say
befehlen	to order	fragen	to ask	mieten	to rent
begegnen	to meet	fühlen	to feel	mitteilen	to inform
beginnen	to begin	führen	to lead	nachsehen	to check
begleiten	to accompany	füllen	to fill	nehmen	to take
bekommen	to receive	geben	to give	nennen	to call
benutzen	to use	gefallen	to please	notieren	to note
beraten	to advise	gehören	to belong	öffnen	to open
beschließen	to decide	gelingen	to succeed	organisieren	to organise
beschreiben	to describe	geschehen	to happen	passieren	to happen
besprechen	to discuss	gewinnen	to win	planen	to plan
bestellen	to order	glauben	to think, believe	plaudern	to chat
besuchen	to visit	haben	to have	raten	to advise
bevorzugen	to prefer	halten	to stop, hold	rechnen	to count
bleiben	to stay	hassen	to hate	reden	to talk
brauchen	to need	heißen	to be called	reparieren	to repair
bringen	to bring	helfen	to help	retten	to save
danken	to thank	hineingehen	to enter	sagen	to say
dauern	to last	hoffen	to hope	schauen	to look
denken	to think	holen	to fetch	scheinen	to seem, shine
drücken	to push	hören	to hear	schenken	to give (gift)
eilen	to hurry	kaufen	to buy	schicken	to send
einkaufen	to shop	kennen	to know	schlagen	to knock, hit
einladen	to invite	kleben	to stick	schließen	to shut
einschalten	to turn on	klettern	to climb	schreiben	to write
einschlafen	to fall asleep	klingeln	to ring	sehen	to see
eintreten	to enter	klopfen	to knock	sich ärgern	to get angry
empfehlen	to recommend	kommen	to come	sich beeilen	to hurry
		kosten	to cost	sich befinden	to be located

Now try this

Pick five verbs at random from each column and see if you can write each one in the present, perfect and future tense for the **ich** form. Check your answers by looking at pages 95–103.

① High frequency language

Verbs S–Z

sich entscheiden	to decide
sich erinnern an	to remember
sich freuen auf	to look forward to
sich langweilen	to get bored
sich streiten	to argue
sitzen	to sit
spazieren	to walk
sprechen	to speak
springen	to jump
stecken	to place
stehlen	to steal
steigen	to climb, get on
stellen	to put
stoppen	to stop
streiten	to argue
studieren	to study at uni
tippen	to type
tragen	to wear, carry
treffen	to meet
trinken	to drink
unterschreiben	to sign
verbessern	to improve
verbringen	to spend (time)
verdienen	to earn
vergeben	to forgive
vergessen	to forget
verhindern	to prevent
verkaufen	to sell
verlassen	to leave
verlieren	to lose
vermeiden	to avoid
versprechen	to promise
verstehen	to understand
versuchen	to try
verzeihen	to forgive
vorbeigehen	to pass by
vorhaben	to intend
vorstellen	to introduce
wählen	to choose, dial
warten auf	to wait for
wechseln	to change
werden	to become
wiederholen	to repeat
wissen	to know
wohnen	to live
wünschen	to wish
zahlen	to pay
zählen	to count
zeigen	to show

fahren   to drive

schlafen   to sleep

gehen   to walk, go

weinen   to cry

essen   to eat

werfen   to throw

zuhören	to listen
zumachen	to close
zurückfahren	to return (by car)
zurückgehen	to return (on foot)
zurückkommen	to come back
zurückstellen	to put back
zusehen	to watch

Modal verbs

dürfen	to be allowed to
können	to be able to
mögen	to like
müssen	to have to
sollen	to be supposed to
wollen	to want to

Adverbs

besonders	especially
da	there
da drüben	over there
dort	there
fast	almost
gern	willingly
hier	here
immer	always, still

irgendwo	somewhere
jedoch	however
leider	unfortunately
lieber	rather
manchmal	sometimes
mehr	more
mitten	in the middle of
neulich	recently
nie	never
oben	above, upstairs
oft	often
regelmäßig	regularly
rückwärts	backwards
schnell	quickly
schon	already
sehr	very
sofort	immediately
unten	below
unterwegs	en route
vielleicht	perhaps
vorwärts	forwards
wahrscheinlich	probably
wirklich	really
ziemlich	rather, quite
zu	too
zusammen	together

Now try this

Choose 20 words you didn't know from this page and the previous page and write them in German. Close the book and try to write the English next to each one. Check back, then test yourself again on any you didn't get right.

① High frequency language

Adjectives A–F

aktuell	current
alle / alles	all
allein	alone
allgemein	general
anders	other
ärgerlich	annoying
artig	well behaved
aufregend	exciting
ausgezeichnet	excellent
bequem	comfortable
bereit	ready
beschäftigt	busy
bestimmt	definite
böse	angry
breit	broad
dankbar	grateful
dicht	dense
draußen	outside
dreckig	dirty
drinnen	inside
dumm	stupid
dynamisch	dynamic
echt	real
ehemalig	old, former
eigen	own
eilig	in a hurry
einzig	only
ekelhaft	disgusting
eng	narrow, tight
erfreut	pleased
ermüdend	tiring
ernst	serious
erschöpft	exhausted
erst	first
erstaunt	astonished
falsch	false
fantastisch	great
faul	lazy
fertig	ready
fleißig	hard-working
flexibel	flexible
frei	free

Adjectives G–N

gebrochen	broken
gefährlich	dangerous
genau	exact
geöffnet	open
geschlossen	closed
gesund	healthy
gleich	similar, same
glücklich	happy
großartig	magnificent
gültig	valid
gut	good
gut gelaunt	in a good mood
hart	severe, unkind / hard, unripe
hässlich	ugly
heiß	hot
hoch	high
hübsch	pretty
jung	young
kaputt	broken
klar	clear
klasse	sensational
komisch	funny
kostenlos	free (cost)
krank	ill
kurz	short
lang	long
langweilig	boring
launisch	moody
laut	noisy
lautlos	silent
leer	empty
leicht	easy
leise	quiet
letzte	last
Lieblings	favourite
lustig	funny
müde	tired
nächst	next
nah	near
nett	kind, nice
neu	new
niedrig	low

Farbe (f)   colour

hell	light
dunkel	dark

blau	
braun	
gelb	
grau	
grün	
lila	
rosa	
rot	
schwarz	
weiß	
gepunktet	
gestreift	

Adjectives N–R

nötig	necessary
notwendig	necessary
nützlich	useful
offen	open
perfekt	perfect
prima	great, marvellous
reich	rich
reif	mature, ripe
richtig	true, right
ruhig	peaceful, calm
rund	round

jung   alt

dick   dünn

groß   klein

Now try this

Look around the room you are in. Try to use 10 German adjectives to describe the room or the objects in it. Then think of a friend you have seen today. Try to use 10 German adjectives to describe their appearance, their personality and their clothing.

① High frequency language

Adjectives S–Z

satt	full
sauber	clean
schlecht	bad
schmal	narrow
schmutzig	dirty
schnell	fast, quick
schön	beautiful
schrecklich	awful, terrible
schüchtern	shy
schwach	weak
schwer	heavy, difficult
schwierig	difficult
spannend	exciting
stark	strong
steil	steep
stolz	proud
streng	strict
teuer	expensive
toll	great
traurig	sad
typisch	typical
überrascht	surprised
umweltfeindlich	eco-unfriendly
umweltfreundlich	eco-friendly
unglaublich	unbelievable
unterschiedlich	variable
unvorstellbar	unimaginable
verantwortlich	responsible
voll	full
wahr	true
weich	soft
weit	far
wertvoll	valuable
wichtig	important
wirklich	real
wunderbar	marvellous
zahlreich	numerous
zornig	angry
zufrieden	pleased, satisfied

Connecting words

aber	but
also	so
auch	also, too
außerdem	moreover
dafür	from that
dann	then
deshalb	for this reason
deswegen	for this reason
nachher	afterwards
oder	or
übrigens	moreover
und	and
vorher	beforehand
zuerst	first of all

Quantities

ein bisschen	a little (of)
ein Drittel	a third of
ein Dutzend	a dozen
ein Glas	a jar of
ein Stück	a piece of
eine Dose	a tin, box of
eine Flasche	a bottle of
eine Packung	a packet of
eine Scheibe	a slice of
eine Tafel	a bar of
eine Tüte	a bag of
genug	enough
mehrere	several
viele	many

Time expressions

ab	from
ab und zu	from time to time
Abend (m)	evening
am Anfang	at the start
bald	soon
früh	early
gestern	yesterday
heute	today
heutzutage	nowadays
immer	always
immer noch	still
jetzt	now
meistens	mostly
Minute (f)	minute
Mittag (m)	midday
Mitternacht (f)	midnight
morgen	tomorrow
Morgen (m)	morning
morgen früh	tomorrow a.m.
Nachmittag (m)	afternoon
nächst	next
Nacht (f)	night
pünktlich	on time
rechtzeitig	on time
seit	since
sofort	immediately
spät	late
später	later
Tag (m)	day
täglich	every day
übermorgen	the day after tomorrow
von Zeit zu Zeit	from time to time
Vormittag (m)	morning
Woche (f)	week
Wochenende (n)	weekend
wöchentlich	weekly

ein kleines
Stück Kuchen

ein großes
Stück Kuchen

ein Glas
Marmelade

eine Tafel
Schokolade

eine Packung
Chips

eine Flasche
Medizin

eine Scheibe
Toast

eine Dose
Erbsen

Now try this

Test yourself on the time expressions above by covering up the English column and then writing down the English translations yourself. Compare your answers with the list above. How many have you got right?

① High frequency language

Questions

wann?	when?
warum?	why?
was?	what?
was für?	what sort of?
wen? wem?	whom? / who?
wer?	who?
wessen?	whose?
wie?	how?
wie viel(e)?	how much / many?
wo?	where?

	Montag Monday	Dienstag Tuesday	Mittwoch Wednesday	Donnerstag Thursday	Freitag Friday	Samstag / Sonnabend Saturday	Sonntag Sunday
07.00							
08.00							

Other high frequency words

alle	everyone
Art (f)	type
das	that
Ding (n)	thing
Ende (n)	end
Form (f)	shape
Frau (f)	Mrs
Gegenstand (m)	object
Herr (m)	Mr
irgendetwas	something
ja	yes
jeder	everybody
jemand	someone
Mal (n)	time
Mitte (f)	middle
nein	no
Nummer (f)	number
ob	whether
Sache (f)	thing
weil	because
Weise (f)	way
wenn	if
wie	as, like
Zahl (f)	figure (number)
zum Beispiel	for example

12-hour clock

Viertel nach zwei   halb drei   zehn vor drei

24-hour clock

 zwölf Uhr fünfundvierzig

 zwanzig Uhr vierzig

 dreiundzwanzig Uhr

Social conventions

alles Gute	all the best	danke schön	thank you
auf Wiedersehen	goodbye	Entschuldigung	excuse me
bis bald	see you soon	grüß Gott	hello
bis morgen	see you tomorrow	gute Nacht	goodnight
		guten Abend	good evening
bis später	see you later	guten Tag	hello, good day
bitte	please		
bitte schön	you're welcome	hallo	hello
		mit bestem Gruß	best wishes
		wie bitte?	pardon?

Months

 Januar

 Februar

 März

 April

 Mai

 Juni

 Juli

 August

 September

 Oktober

 November

 Dezember

Now try this

Practise the days of the week and the months of the year by translating the birthdays of family and friends into German.

① High frequency language

Prepositions

an	at
auf	on
aus	out of
außer	except
bei	with, at (house)
bis	until
durch	through
entlang	along
für	for
gegen	towards
gegenüber	opposite
hinter	behind
in	in, into
mit	with
nach	after
neben	next to
ohne	without
seit	since
statt	instead of
trotz	despite
über	above, over
um	around
unter	beneath, under
von	from
vor	in front of
während	during
wegen	because of
zu	to
zwischen	between

Continents

Afrika	Africa
Asien	Asia
Australien	Australia
Europa	Europe
Nordamerika	North America
Südamerika	South America

Countries

Belgien	Belgium
Dänemark	Denmark
Griechenland	Greece
Indien	India
die Niederlande	Netherlands
Russland	Russia
Deutschland	
die Schweiz	
die Türkei	
die Vereinigten Staaten	
England	
Frankreich	
Großbritannien	
Irland	
Italien	
Österreich	
Schottland	
Spanien	
Wales	

Nationalities

The first line of each entry in this secti... is the noun (a German man / woman, etc.). The second line is the adjective.

Afrikaner/in afrikanisch	African
Amerikaner/in amerikanisch	American
Belgier/in belgisch	Belgian
Brite/Britin britisch	British
Däne/Dänin dänisch	Danish
Deutsche(r) deutsch	German
Engländer/in englisch	English
Europäer/in europäisch	European
Franzose/Französin französisch	French
Grieche/Griechin griechisch	Greek
Ire/Irin irisch	Irish
Italiener/in italienisch	Italian
Niederländer/in niederländisch	Dutch
Österreicher/in österreichisch	Austrian
Russe/Russin russisch	Russian
Schotte/Schottin schottisch	Scottish
Schweizer/in schweizerisch	Swiss
Spanier/in spanisch	Spanish
Waliser/in walisisch	Welsh

Now try this

Match the German place names to their English equivalents.

(a)	Bayern	Vienna
(b)	der Ärmelkanal	Bavaria
(c)	der Bodensee	Geneva
(d)	der Schwarzwald	Danube
(e)	die Alpen	Black Forest
(f)	die Donau	Cologne
(g)	Genf	English Channel
(h)	Köln	Lake Constance
(i)	München	Munich
(j)	Wien	Alps

② Identity and culture

Food and drink

Zitrone (f)   Ananas (f)   Apfel (m)   Birne (f)   Erdbeere (f)

Kirsche (f)   Pflaume (f)   Karotte (f)   Champignon / Pilz (m)

Erbsen (pl)   Paprika (f)   Kartoffel (f)   Tomate (f)

Abendessen (n)	evening meal
Apfelsine (f)	orange
Appetit (m)	appetite
Aprikose (f)	apricot
Aufschnitt (m)	cold sliced meat
Auswahl (f)	choice, selection
bedienen	to serve
Besteck (n)	cutlery
bestellen	to order
bezahlen	to pay
Blumenkohl (m)	cauliflower
Bockwurst (f)	frankfurter
Bohne (f)	bean
Braten (m)	roast
Bratwurst (f)	fried sausage
Brot (n)	bread
Brötchen (n)	roll
Butterbrot (n)	sandwich
Champagner (m)	champagne
Chips (pl)	crisps
Ei (n)	egg
Eisdiele (f)	ice cream parlour
Erfrischungen (pl)	refreshments
Essig (m)	vinegar
Fertiggericht (n)	ready meal
Fleisch (n)	meat
Frikadelle (f)	meatball
Fruchtsaft (m)	fruit juice
Frühstück (n)	breakfast
Gabel (f)	fork
Gasthaus (n)	inn
Gebäck (n)	pastries
Geld (n)	money
gemischt	mixed
Gemüse (n)	vegetables
Getränk (n)	drink
Gurke (f)	cucumber
Hähnchen (n)	chicken
Hauptgericht (n)	main course
Himbeere (f)	raspberry
hungrig	hungry
Imbissstube (f)	snack bar
Kakao (m)	cocoa
Kännchen (n)	pot
Käse (m)	cheese
Kebab (m) / Döner (m)	kebab
Keks (m)	biscuit
Kellner (m) / Kellnerin (f)	waiter / waitress
Kohl (m)	cabbage
Kotelett (n)	chop (e.g. pork)
Krapfen (m)	doughnut

Kuchen (m)	cake
Leberwurst (f)	liver sausage
lecker	tasty
Löffel (m)	spoon
Mahlzeit (f)	meal
Marmelade (f)	jam
Menü (n)	set meal
Messer (n)	knife
Milch (f)	milk
Mineralwasser (n)	mineral water
Mittagessen (n)	lunch
Nachspeise (f)	dessert
Nachtisch (m)	dessert
Nudeln (pl)	pasta
Obst (n)	fruit
Obsttorte (f)	fruit pie
Pfirsich (m)	peach
Pommes (frites) (pl)	chips
probieren	to try
Rechnung (f)	bill
Rindfleisch (n)	beef
roh	raw
Ruhetag (m)	day off
Saft (m)	juice
Sahne (f)	cream
Salat (m)	lettuce, salad
Salz (n)	salt
satt	full up
scharf	hot (spicy)
Schinken (m)	ham
Schnellimbiss (m)	snack bar
Schnitzel (n)	escalope
Schokolade (f)	chocolate
Schweinefleisch (n)	pork
Selbstbedienung (f)	self-service
Senf (m)	mustard
Soße (f)	gravy, sauce
Speisekarte (f)	menu
Speisesaal (m)	dining room
Spezialität (f)	speciality
Steak (n)	steak
Suppe (f)	soup
süß	sweet
Tagesgericht (n)	dish of the day
Tasse (f)	cup
Teelöffel (m)	teaspoon
Teller (m)	plate

Thunfisch (m)	tuna
Tisch (m)	table
Tischtuch (n)	tablecloth
Torte (f)	gateau
trinken	to drink
Trinkgeld (n)	tip (money)
Vegetarier/in (m/f)	vegetarian (person)
vegetarisch	vegetarian (food)
voll	full
Vorspeise (f)	starter
Wein (m)	wine
Weintraube (f)	grape
Wurst (f)	sausage
Zucker (m)	sugar
Zwiebel (f)	onion

HIGHER

Bier vom Fass (n)	draught beer
blutig	rare (steak)
durch	well-done (steak)
Ente (f)	duck
Forelle (f)	trout
gedämpft, gedünstet	steamed
geräuchert	smoked
hausgemacht	home-made
Honig (m)	honey
Kalbfleisch (n)	veal
Knoblauch (m)	garlic
Kräutertee (m)	herbal tea
Lachs (m)	salmon
Meeresfrüchte (pl)	seafood
Pute (f)	turkey
Rührei (n)	scrambled egg
scharf	sharp, spicy
schmackhaft	tasty
Sekt (m)	sparkling wine
Spiegelei (n)	fried egg
Spinat (m)	spinach
Tablett (n)	tray
Truthahn (m)	turkey
Untertasse (f)	saucer
Vollmilch (f)	full-fat milk
würzig, pikant	spicy

Now try this

Look at the pictures on this page and memorise the items. Then close the book and see how many you can remember – in German! Open the book and check your spelling carefully.

② Identity and culture

Dress and style

altmodisch	old-fashioned
angezogen	dressed
Anzug (m)	suit
Armband (n)	bracelet
Badeanzug (m)	swimming costume
Badehose (f)	trunks
aus Baumwolle	in cotton
gepflegt, schick	smart
Halskette (f)	necklace
Halstuch (n)	scarf
Handschuh (m)	glove
Juwelen (pl)	jewels
Klamotten (pl)	clothes (slang)
Kleidung (f)	clothing
Lippenstift (m)	lipstick
Marke (f)	make, brand
Mode (f)	fashion
modisch	fashionable
Mütze (f)	cap
Nachthemd (n)	nightdress
Ohrring (m)	earring
Pantoffel (m)	slipper
Pullover, Pulli (m)	pullover
Regenschirm (m)	umbrella
Schlafanzug (m)	pyjamas
Schlips (m)	tie
Schminke (f)	make-up
Slip (m)	pants, briefs
Stiefel (m)	boot
Strumpfhose (f)	tights
Trainingsanzug (m)	tracksuit
Unterhose (f)	underpants

eng	tight
gefärbt	dyed
Morgenmantel (m)	dressing gown
aus Seide / Samt	made from silk / velvet
sich schminken	to put on make-up
Wolljacke (f)	cardigan

Gürtel (m)

Kleid (n)

Schal (m)

Hemd (n)

Krawatte (f) / Schlips (m)

Schuh (m)

Hut (m)

Rock (m)

Socke (f)

Bluse (f)

Jacke (f)

Jeans (f)

Mantel (m)

Shorts (pl)

Sportschuhe (pl)

Family, friends and home

allein	alone	Besuch (m)	visit
alt	old	besuchen	to visit
älter	older	bevorzugen	to prefer
Alter (n)	age	Beziehung (f)	relationship
arbeitslos	unemployed	Bild (n)	picture
arm	poor	blöd	foolish, silly
auf die Nerven gehen	to annoy	böse	angry, cross
Augen (pl)	eyes	Brieffreund (m)	penfriend
auskommen mit	to get on with	Brille (f)	glasses
aussehen	to look (appearance)	Bruder (m)	brother
babysitten	to babysit	charmant	charming
Badezimmer (n)	bathroom	Cousin/e (m/f)	cousin
Bart (m)	beard	Doppelhaus (n)	semi-detached house
bequem, gemütlich	comfortable, cosy	egoistisch	selfish
berühmt	famous	Ehe (f)	marriage
		Ehemann (m)	husband
		Ehering (m)	wedding ring

Now try this

Think of all the clothes items on this page that you have worn during the past week. Make a list in English then try to write the German equivalents without looking at the page. Check back to see how many you got right. Learn the ones you got wrong!

② Identity and culture

German	English	German	English	German	English
ehrlich	honest	heißen	to be called	Postleitzahl (f)	postcode
einladen	to invite	Hochzeit (f)	wedding	Prominente (m/f)	celebrity
Einladung (f)	invitation	höflich	polite	rechthaberisch	bossy
einsam	lonely	hübsch	pretty	reich	rich
einverstanden	agreed	humorlos	no sense of humour	Reihenhaus (n)	terraced house
Einzelkind (n)	only child			Respekt haben vor	to respect
Eltern (pl)	parents	humorvoll	humorous	sauer	sour, cross
Enkelkind (n)	grandchild	Hund (m)	dog	Schlafzimmer (n)	bedroom
ernst	serious	Jahr (n)	year	schlank	thin
Erwachsene (m/f)	adult	Jugend (f)	youth (time of life)	Schnurrbart (m)	moustache
Esszimmer (n)	dining room			schön	beautiful
Familie (f)	family	Jugendliche (m/f)	young person	schüchtern	shy
Feier (f)	party	jung	young	schwätzen	to chat
feiern	to celebrate	Junge (m)	boy	Schwester (f)	sister
Frau (f)	wife, woman	Katze (f)	cat	Schwiegersohn (m) /-tochter (f)	son / daughter-in-law
frech	cheeky	kennen	to know		
Freund (m)	male friend	Kind (n)	child		
Freundin (f)	female friend	klug, intelligent	intelligent	selbst	self
freundlich	friendly	komisch	funny (strange)	Sessel (m)	armchair
Freundschaft (f)	friendship	kritisieren	to criticise	sich freuen auf	to look forward to
Garten (m)	garden	Küche (f)	kitchen		
Garage (f)	garage	Kuss (m)	kiss	sich kümmern um	to look after
geboren	born	küssen	to kiss	sich streiten	to argue
Geburtsdatum (n)	date of birth	Laune (f)	mood	sich trennen	to separate
Geburtsort (m)	birthplace	Leben (n)	life	sich verloben	to get engaged
Geburtstag (m)	birthday	lebendig	lively		
geduldig	patient	ledig	unmarried	sich verstehen	to get on
Gefühl (n)	feeling	leiden	to suffer, bear	sich vorstellen	to introduce
gemein	mean, nasty	nicht leiden können	to dislike, not be able to bear	Sohn (m)	son
gern haben	to like			sorgen für	to care for
Geschenk (n)	present			spenden	to donate
geschieden	divorced	Leute (pl)	people	Spitzname (m)	nickname
Geschwister (pl)	siblings	lieb	likeable	Stief-	step-
Gesicht (n)	face	lockig	curly	still	quiet
gesprächig, schwatzhaft	chatty	lustig	funny	Streit (m)	argument
		Mädchen (n)	girl	Stuhl (m)	chair
getrennt	separated	Mann (m)	man, husband	sympathisch	nice, likeable
glatt	straight (hair)	Meerschweinchen (n)	guinea pig	Tante (f)	aunt
eine Glatze haben	to be bald			Tochter (f)	daughter
gratulieren	to congratulate	Möbel (pl)	furniture	tot	dead
		multikulturell, multikulti	multicultural	Traum (m)	dream
großartig	magnificent			traurig	sad
Großeltern (pl)	grandparents	Mund (m)	mouth	Typ (m)	guy, bloke
Großmutter (f)	grandmother	Mutter (f)	mother	Umfrage (f)	survey
Großvater (m)	grandfather	Nachbar (m)	neighbour	unerträglich	unbearable
gut / schlecht gelaunt	in a good / bad mood	nett	nice, kind	unternehmungslustig	adventurous
		Oma (f)	grandma		
Haar (n)	hair	Onkel (m)	uncle	unterstützen	to support
Halb-	half-	Opa (m)	grandad	Vater (m)	father
hässlich	ugly	ordentlich	tidy	verheiratet	married
Haus (n)	house	Person (f) / Mensch (m)	person	verliebt	in love
Haustier (n)	pet			verlobt	engaged
Heim (n)	home	Persönlichkeit (f)	personality	Vorname (m)	first name
heiraten	to get married	pessimistisch	pessimistic	Wohnblock (m)	block of flats
		Piercing (n)	body piercing	Wohnort (m)	home location

Now try this

To help you learn the personality adjectives, write out the German words in three lists: positive, negative and neutral. Then memorise five adjectives that could describe you.

② Identity and culture

Wohnung (f)	flat
Wohnzimmer (n)	sitting room
zufrieden	satisfied
Zuhause (n)	home
Zwillinge (pl)	twins

ähnlich	similar
Alleinerziehende (m/f)	single parent
Alleinstehende (m/f)	single person
(hohes) Alter (n)	old age
Altersheim (n)	old people's home
angeberisch	pretentious
ausgeglichen, ausgewogen	well-balanced
aussehen wie	to resemble
benachteiligen	to disadvantage
leiden	to suffer
minderjährig	underage
Pickel (m)	spot (acne)
rassistisch	racist
Rentner/in (m/f)	pensioner
schikanieren, mobben	to bully
selbstsicher, selbstbewusst	self-confident
sensibel, empfindlich	sensitive
stur, dickköpfig	stubborn
Treffen (n)	meeting
verständnisvoll	understanding
Verwandte (m/f)	relative
verwöhnt, verdorben	spoilt
Vorbild (n)	role model
zuverlässig	reliable

Lifestyle: healthy living and exercise

abnehmen	to lose weight
Alkohol (m)	alcohol
alkoholisch	alcoholic

alt	old
Alter (n)	age
Angst haben	to be afraid
Arm (m)	arm
atmen	to breathe
aufgeben	to give up
aufhören	to stop
Bauch (m)	stomach
Bein (n)	leg
betrunken	drunk
brechen	to break
Diät machen	to diet
dick	fat
Droge (f)	drug
dünn	thin
Durchfall (m)	diarrhoea
Durst (m)	thirst
durstig	thirsty
Erkältung (f)	cold
Erste Hilfe	first aid
fettig	fatty, greasy
Fieber (n)	temperature
Finger (m)	finger
Fuß (m)	foot
gebrochen	broken
gesund	healthy
Gesundheit (f)	health
glücklich	happy
Grippe (f)	flu
Hals (m)	neck, throat
Hand (f)	hand
Herz (n)	heart
husten	to cough
Knie (n)	knee
Kopf (m)	head
Körper (m)	body
köstlich	delicious
laufen	to run
lebendig	lively
Leber (f)	liver
Lunge (f)	lung
Magen (m)	stomach
mager	low-fat
Medikament (n)	medicine
nervös	nervous
rauchen	to smoke
Raucher (m)	smoker
riechen	to smell
Rücken (m)	back (body)
Ruhe (f)	calm, peace
schlimm	bad
schmecken	to taste
Schmerz (m)	pain
Schulter (f)	shoulder
sich entspannen	to relax
sich fit halten	to keep fit

sich fühlen	to feel
sich verletzen	to harm, injure
sportlich	sporty
Spritze (f)	injection
spritzen	to inject
sterben	to die
stressig	stressful
übel	sick, ill
Unfall (m)	accident
ungesund	unhealthy
Vegetarier/in (m/f)	vegetarian
Verletzung (f)	injury
Verstopfung (f)	constipation
vorbereiten	to prepare
weh tun	to hurt
Zahn (m)	tooth
Zigarette (f)	cigarette
zunehmen	to put on weight

abhängig	addicted
Ballaststoff (m)	dietary fibre
Behandlung (f)	treatment
bewusstlos	unconscious
Biokost (f)	organic food
Blut (n)	blood
Entziehungskur (f)	rehab
ermüdend	tiring
fettarm	low-fat
Fettleibigkeit (f)	obesity
Fußgelenk (n)	ankle
Gehirn (n)	brain
Geruch (m)	smell
Geschmack (m)	taste
Heuschnupfen (m)	hay fever
Krebs (m)	cancer
magersüchtig	anorexic
Mehl (n)	flour
Nahrung (f)	food
Nuss (f)	nut
Rauschgift (n)	drug(s)
Schnupfen (m)	cold
schwindlig	dizzy
sich erholen	to recover
sich gewöhnen an	to get used to
sich trimmen	to keep fit
Sucht (f)	addiction
süchtig	addicted
übergewichtig	overweight
verstauchen	to sprain

Now try this

Write at least 10 body parts in German from memory. Look at the page and check your spelling.

② Identity and culture

Cultural life

Ich spiele ...
I play ...

Geige (f)　Trompete (f)　Flöte (f)

Schlagzeug (n)

Klarinette (f)　Klavier (n)　Blockflöte (f)

Agentenroman (m)	spy novel
Bräutigam (m)	bridegroom
Buch (n)	book
Bühne (f)	stage
Computerspiel (n)	computer game
Disko / Disco (f)	disco
Dokumentarfilm (m)	documentary
Dreikönigsfest (n)	Epiphany
Ehe (f)	marriage
Ehering (m)	wedding ring
Fantasyfilm (m)	fantasy film
Fastenzeit (f)	Lent
Feier / Party (f)	party
Fernsehkanal (m)	TV channel
Fotoapparat (m)	camera
Freizeit (f)	free time, leisure
Freizeitbeschäftigung (f)	leisure activity
gratulieren	to congratulate
Gruppe / Band (f)	band
Handy (n)	mobile phone
Heiligabend (m)	Christmas Eve
heiraten	to get married
Hobby (n)	hobby
Hochzeit (f)	wedding
Horrorfilm (m)	horror film
Jugendklub (m)	youth club
Karfreitag (m)	Good Friday
Kino (n)	cinema
Konzert (n)	concert
Krimi (m)	detective story
Lesen (n)	reading
Liebesfilm (m)	love film
Lied (n)	song
MP3-Datei (f)	MP3 file
Muttertag (m)	Mother's Day
Nachrichten (pl)	news

Neujahr (n)	New Year
Ostermontag (m)	Easter Monday
Ostern (n)	Easter
Popmusik (f)	pop music
Quizsendung (f)	quiz show
romantisch	romantic
sammeln	to collect
Sammlung (f)	collection
Sänger/in (m/f)	singer
Schau (f)	show
Seifenoper (f)	soap opera
Sender (m)	(TV) channel
Sendung (f)	(TV) programme
Serie (f)	series
Silvester (n)	New Year's Eve
Spielkonsole (f)	games console
Spielzeug (n)	toy
Spionageroman (m)	spy novel
Taschengeld (n)	pocket money
Theaterstück (n)	play
Unterhaltung (f)	entertainment
Vergnügen (n)	pleasure
Volksmusik (f)	folk music
Weihnachten (n)	Christmas
Wettbewerb (m)	competition
Zeichentrickfilm (m)	cartoon
Zeitschrift (f)	magazine

Brettspiel (n)	board game
Fernbedienung (f)	remote control
Fernsehkomödie (f)	sitcom
Heimwerken (n)	DIY
Hochzeitsfeier (f)	wedding ceremony
Melodie (f)	melody, tune
Originalfassung (f)	original version

Publikum (n)	audience
Satellitenfernsehen (n)	satellite TV
synchronisiert	dubbed
Untertitel (pl)	subtitles
Verlobung (f)	engagement (pre-marriage)
Wissen (n)	knowledge
Zuhörer (m/pl)	listener(s)
Zuschauer (m/pl)	viewer(s)

Cultural life (sports)

(asiatische) Kampfsportarten (pl)	martial arts
Ausrüstung (f)	equipment
Bergsteigen (n)	mountaineering
Bodybuilding (n)	bodybuilding
Bogenschießen (n)	archery
Boxen (n)	boxing
bummeln	to go for a stroll
Extremsport (m)	extreme sport
Fallschirmspringen (n)	parachuting
Fan (m)	fan (supporter)
Federball (m)	badminton
Fußball (m)	football
Gleitschirmfliegen (n)	paragliding
Halle (f)	hall
Handball (m)	handball
Hockey (n)	hockey
Inlineskaten (n)	rollerblading
Judo (n)	judo
Kanufahren (n)	canoeing
Karate (n)	karate

Now try this

Choose five compound nouns from this page and write them as their separate nouns. That way you can expand your vocabulary!

② Identity and culture

kegeln gehen	to go bowling
Klettern (n)	climbing
Mannschaft (f)	team
Mitglied (n)	member
Radfahren (n)	cycling
reiten	to ride a horse
Rollschuh laufen	to rollerskate
Schach (n)	chess
Schiedsrichter (m)	referee
Schlittschuhlaufen (n)	ice skating
Schwimmen (n)	swimming
Segeln (n)	sailing
Skateboard fahren (n)	to go skateboarding
spazieren gehen	to go for a stroll
Spiel (n)	game
Sport (m), Sportart (f)	sport
sportlich	sporty
Sportplatz (m)	sports ground
Sport treiben	to do sport
Surfen (n)	surfing
Tanz (m), Tanzen (n)	dance, dancing
teilnehmen an	to take part in
Tennis (n)	tennis
Tischtennis (n)	table tennis
ein Tor schießen	to score a goal
trainieren	to exercise
Trampolinspringen (n)	trampolining
Turnen (n), Gymnastik (f)	gymnastics
Verein (m)	club
wandern	to hike
Wasserskifahren (n)	waterskiing
Windsurfen (n)	windsurfing

Bildschirm (m)	screen
Tastatur (f)	keyboard
Taste (f)	key
Drucker (m)	printer
Computer (m)	computer

HIGHER H

Angelrute (f)	fishing rod
Fechten (n)	fencing
Halbzeit (f)	half time
Liga (f)	league
Meisterschaft (f)	championship
Rudern (n)	rowing
Segelboot (n)	sailing boat
Sporttauchen (n)	scuba diving
Turnier (n)	tournament
Umkleidekabine (f)	changing rooms

Using social media

FOUNDATION Fn

Anschluss (m)	connection
Blog (m/n)	blog
brennen	to burn
Chatroom (m), Chatraum (m)	chatroom
chatten	to chat (online)
Computervirus (m/n)	computer virus
E-Mail (f)	email
drucken	to print
Festplatte (f)	disk
Gefahr (f)	danger

herunterladen, downloaden	to download
hochladen, heraufladen, uploaden	to upload
Homepage (f)	homepage
Internet-Mobbing (f)	cyberbullying
Internetseite (f)	website, web page
mailen	to email
löschen	to delete, remove
Passwort (n)	password
Progammierer (m), Programmiererin (f)	programmer
Schrägstrich (m)	forward slash
Sicherheit (f)	security
sichern, speichern, absaven	to save, store
soziales Netzwerk (n)	social network
tippen	to type
Verbindung (f)	connection
Web (n)	web
Webcam (f), Netzkamera (f)	webcam
Website / Webseite (f)	website, web page

Now try this

Make two lists of the sports from this page and page 119: ones you have played and ones you have never played.

❸ Local area, holiday and travel

Local area

das Stadion — the stadium

der Flughafen — the airport

die Post — the post office

der Dom — the cathedral

der Bahnhof — the railway station

Abfalleimer (m)	rubbish bin
Apotheke (f)	chemist's
Bäckerei (f)	baker's
Bauernhof (m)	farm
Bibliothek (f)	library
Buchhandlung (f)	bookshop
Busbahnhof (m)	bus station
Eishalle (f)	ice rink
Fabrik (f)	factory
Freizeitpark (m)	theme park
Freizeitzentrum (n)	leisure centre
Gebäude (n)	building
Geschäft (n)	shop
Hafen (m)	port
Hallenbad (n)	indoor pool
Hochhaus (n)	tower block
Kaufhaus (n)	department store
Kino (n)	cinema
Kirche (f)	church
Kneipe (f)	pub
Krankenhaus (n)	hospital
Kunstgalerie (f)	art gallery
Laden (m)	shop
Lebensmittelgeschäft (n)	grocer's
Markt (m)	market
Metzgerei (f)	butcher's
Museum (n)	museum
Nachtklub (m)	nightclub
Palast (m)	palace
Platz (m)	square
Polizeiwache (f)	police station
Rathaus (n)	town hall
Schloss (n)	castle
Schnellimbiss (m)	snack bar
Schwimmbad (n)	swimming pool
Spielplatz (m)	playground

Sportzentrum (n)	sports centre
Supermarkt (m)	supermarket
Tankstelle (f)	petrol station
Treffpunkt (m)	meeting place
Turm (m)	tower
Unterhaltungsmöglichkeiten (pl)	entertainment, things to do
Waschsalon (m)	launderette
Zeitungskiosk (m)	news kiosk

Denkmal (n)	monument
Flohmarkt (m)	flea market
Geldautomat (m)	cashpoint
Grünanlage (f)	park
Reinigung (f)	dry cleaner's

Holiday accommodation

ankommen	to arrive
Ankunft (f)	arrival
Anmeldung (f)	booking in
Aufenthaltsraum (m)	games room
Aufzug (m)	lift
Ausgang (m)	exit
auspacken	to unpack
Aussicht (f)	view
Bad (n)	bath
Badetuch (n)	towel
Badewanne (f)	bathtub

Badezimmer (n)	bathroom
Balkon (m)	balcony
besetzt	occupied
Besitzer (m)	owner
Betttuch (n)	sheet
Bettwäsche (f)	bed linen
Campingplatz (m)	campsite
Doppelzimmer (n)	double room
Dorf (n)	village
Dusche (f)	shower
Einzelzimmer (n)	single room
Empfang (m)	reception
Erdgeschoss (n)	ground floor
Esszimmer (n)	dining room
Etage (f)	floor (1st, 2nd)
Fahrstuhl (m)	lift
Fenster (n)	window
Fernsehapparat (n)	TV set
frei	free, available
funktionieren	to work
Gepäck (n)	luggage
Halbpension (f)	half board
Heizung (f)	heating
Hotelverzeichnis (n)	hotel list
im ersten Stock	on the first floor
im Voraus	in advance
inbegriffen	included
Jugendherberge (f)	youth hostel
Kleiderschrank (m)	wardrobe
Koffer (m)	suitcase
Kopfkissen (n)	pillow
Küche (f)	kitchen
Miete (f)	rent
mieten	to rent
mit Blick auf	with a view of

Now try this

Without looking at the book, think about all of the amenities in your local town or city and make a list of them in German. Open the book and then check your spelling.

③ Local area, holiday and travel

möbliert	furnished
Pension (f)	B& B
Preisliste (f)	price list
Reservierung (f)	reservation
Schlafsack (m)	sleeping bag
Schlafzimmer (n)	bedroom
Schlüssel (m)	key
Seife (f)	soap
Stock (m)	floor (1st, 2nd)
Treppe (f)	staircase
Trinkwasser (n)	drinking water
übernachten	to stay the night
Übernachtung (f)	overnight stay
Untergeschoss (n)	basement
Unterkunft (f)	accommodation
Vollpension (f)	full board
Wand (f)	wall (inside)
Waschbecken (n)	wash basin
Wohnwagen (m)	caravan
Wohnzimmer (n)	sitting room
Zahnbürste (f)	toothbrush
Zahnpasta (f)	toothpaste
Zelt (n)	tent
zelten	to camp (tent)
Zweibettzimmer (n)	twin room

bestätigen	to confirm
Gastfreundschaft (f)	hospitality
Klimaanlage (f)	air conditioning
Notausgang (m)	emergency exit
unterbringen	to put someone up

Visitor information

Andenken (n)	souvenir
Ausflug (m)	outing
Ausgang (m)	exit
Ausstellung (f)	exhibition
Berg (m)	mountain
Broschüre (f)	brochure
Bürgersteig (m)	pavement
Büro (n)	office
Dorf (n)	village
draußen	outside
Eingang (m)	entrance
Eintrittsgeld (n)	admission
Einwohner (m)	inhabitant
Ermäßigung (f)	reduction
Feiertag (m)	public holiday
Feld (n)	field
Fest (n)	festival
flach	flat
Fußgänger (m)	pedestrian
Gegend (f)	area
geöffnet	open
geschlossen	closed
Hauptstadt (f)	capital city
Hügel (m)	hill
im Ausland	abroad
im Freien	in the open air
im Frühling	in spring
im Herbst	in autumn
im Sommer	in summer
im Winter	in winter
Informationsbüro (n)	information office
Insel (f)	island
Küste (f)	coast
Land (n)	country
Landschaft (f)	countryside
malerisch	picturesque
Meer (n)	sea
Öffnungszeiten (pl)	opening hours
Ort (m)	place

ruhig	quiet
Rundfahrt (f)	tour
Rundgang (m)	tour (walking)
Schild (n)	sign
See (f)	sea
See (m)	lake
sehenswert	worth seeing
Sehenswürdigkeiten (pl)	sights
Stadt (f)	town
Stadtplan (m)	town map
Stadtrand (m)	outskirts
Stadtteil (m)	part of town
Stadtviertel (n)	district
Stadtzentrum (n)	town centre
Strand (m)	beach
Verkehrsamt (n)	tourist office
Vorort (m)	suburb
Vorstellung (f)	performance
Wald (m)	wood, forest

Aufenthalt (m)	stay
Badeort (m)	seaside resort
Bodensee (m)	Lake Constance
Brunnen (m)	fountain
Erinnerung (f)	memory
Erlebnis (n)	experience
Feuerwerk (n)	firework
Gebiet (n)	area
Grünanlage (f)	park
Lärm (m)	noise
Pauschalreise (f)	package holiday
stattfinden	to take place
Tiergarten (m)	zoo
Umgebung (f)	surrounding area
Umzug (m)	procession
Veranstaltung (f)	event
Zoll (m)	customs

Now try this

Choose five words from this page which are important to you on a holiday. Write a sentence for each word in German.

❸ Local area, holiday and travel

Travel (transport)

Foundation

Abfahrt (f)	departure
Abflug (m)	plane departure
Abgase (pl)	exhaust fumes
Abteil (n)	compartment
Ankunft (f)	arrival
Anschluss (m)	connection
aussteigen	to get off
Autobahn (f)	motorway
Bahn (f)	railway
Bahnsteig (m)	platform
Benzin (n)	petrol
einfach	single (ticket)
Einfahrt (f)	entrance (road)
einsteigen	to get on (train)
Einzelfahrkarte (f)	single ticket
entwerten	to validate ticket
Fähre (f)	ferry
Fahrkarte (f)	ticket
Fahrplan (m)	timetable
Fahrt (f)	journey, trip

Führerschein (m)	driving licence
Gepäckaufbewahrung (f)	left luggage
Gleis (n)	platform
Haltestelle (f)	stop (bus, train)
hin und zurück	return (ticket)
Karte (f)	ticket
Motor (m)	engine
öffentliche Verkehrsmittel	public transport
Panne (f)	breakdown
Platz (m)	seat
Reise (f)	journey
Rückfahrkarte (f)	return ticket
S-Bahn (f)	suburban train
schaden	to harm
schädlich	harmful
Schalter (m)	counter
Schlafwagen (m)	sleeper
Schließfach (n)	luggage locker
sich verspäten	to be late
Stau (m)	traffic jam
Straßenkarte (f)	road map
Tankstelle (f)	petrol station
U-Bahn (f)	underground railway
Überfahrt (f)	crossing

Umleitung (f)	diversion
umsteigen	to change
Verbindung (f)	connection
Verkehr (m)	traffic
verpassen	to miss
Verspätung (f)	delay
Vorfahrt (f)	priority
Wagen (m)	car, carriage
Wartesaal (m)	waiting room

Higher

Autobahnkreuz (n)	motorway junction
bremsen	to brake
Fahrzeug (n)	vehicle
Geschwindigkeit (f)	speed
Hubschrauber (m)	helicopter
Raststätte (f)	motorway services
sich beeilen	to hurry
Sicherheitsgurt (m)	safety belt
Stoßzeit (f)	rush hour
überholen	to overtake

Auto (n)

Zug (m)

Boot (n)

Bus (m)

Fahrrad (n)

Flugzeug (n)

Lastwagen (m)

Mofa (n)

Motorrad (n)

Straßenbahn (f)

Now try this

Make a list of all the forms of transport you have used in the past year. Memorise the words then test yourself on the German spellings.

❸ Local area, holiday and travel

Travel (directions)

 (Foundation)

Ampel (f)	traffic lights
Brücke (f)	bridge
Ecke (f)	corner
Einbahnstraße (f)	one-way street
Fluss (m)	river
Kreisverkehr (m)	roundabout
Kreuzung (f)	crossroads
Landkarte (f)	map
Richtung (f)	direction
sich befinden	to be situated
überqueren	to cross
weit	far
zu Fuß	on foot

 auf der linken Seite — on the left

 auf der rechten Seite — on the right

 links — left

 rechts — right

geradeaus — straight on

Weather

(Foundation)

bedeckt	overcast
bewölkt	cloudy
es donnert	it's thundering

es friert	it's freezing
frostig	frosty
Gewitter (n), Sturm (m)	thunderstorm
Grad (m)	degree
heiß	hot
heiter	bright
Himmel (m)	sky
Hitze (f)	heat
Höchsttemperatur (f)	highest temperature
Jahreszeit (f)	season
kalt	cold
Klima (n)	climate
nass	wet
neblig	foggy
Regen (m)	rain
regnerisch	rainy
schlecht	bad
Schnee (m)	snow
sonnig	sunny
Sturm (m)	storm
Tiefsttemperatur (f)	lowest temperature
trocken	dry
Wolke (f)	cloud
wolkig	cloudy

 die Sonne scheint

 es ist windig

 es schneit

 es blitzt

 es regnet

es ist kalt

im Norden
im Westen — im Osten
im Süden

(Higher)

Aufheiterung (f)	bright spell
aufklären	to brighten up
Durchschnitts- temperatur (f)	average temperature
hageln	to hail
Niederschlag (m)	rainfall
stürmisch	stormy
wechselhaft	changeable

Dealing with problems

(Foundation)

Bedienung (f)	service
Beschwerde (f)	complaint
Diebstahl (m)	theft
Ersatzteil (n)	replacement part
ersetzen	to replace
Farbe (f)	colour
Fehler (m)	mistake, fault
Formular (n)	form
kaputt	broken
Kundendienst (m)	customer service
Lieferung (f)	delivery
Menge (f)	quantity
Panne (f)	breakdown
Quittung (f)	receipt
Rechnung (f)	bill (invoice)
Reparatur (f)	repair
reparieren	to repair
Schaden (m)	damage
sich beschweren	to complain
umtauschen	to exchange
Unfall (m)	accident
Wartezeit (f)	waiting time
zahlen	to pay

(Higher)

(Auto)unfall (m)	crash / collision
Gebrauchsanweisung (f)	instructions for use
versichern	to insure
Versicherung (f)	insurance

Now try this

Test this vocabulary, and your knowledge of tenses, by trying to describe the weather yesterday, the weather today, and what you hope the weather will be like tomorrow.

④ School

FOUNDATION Fn

Abitur (n)	equivalent of A levels
abwesend	absent
anwesend	present
Aula (f)	school hall
Austausch (m)	exchange
Berufsberater/in (m/f)	careers adviser
bestehen	to pass (exam)
Bildung (f)	education
Biologie (f)	biology
Bleistift (m)	pencil
Chemie (f)	chemistry
Chor (m)	choir
dauern	to last
Deutsch	German
Direktor (m), Schulleiter (m)	head teacher
durchfallen	to fail (exam)
Englisch	English
Erdkunde (f)	geography
Erfolg (m)	success
erfolgreich	successful
Etui (n)	pencil case
Fach (n)	subject
faul	lazy
Ferien (pl)	holidays
Filzstift (m)	felt tip
fleißig	hard-working
Fortschritt (m)	progress
Frage (f)	question
Französisch	French
Fremdsprachen (pl)	languages
Füller (m)	fountain pen
Gang (m)	corridor
gerecht	fair
Gesamtschule (f)	comprehensive school
Geschichte (f)	history
Grundschule (f)	primary school
Gymnasium (n)	grammar school
Hauptschule / Realschule (f)	secondary school
Hausaufgaben (pl)	homework
Hausmeister (m)	caretaker
Heft (n)	exercise book
Informatik (f)	ICT
Kantine (f)	canteen
Klassenarbeit (f)	class test
Klassenfahrt (f)	school trip
Klassenzimmer (n)	classroom
Klebstoff (m)	glue

klug	clever
korrigieren	to correct
Kuli (m)	ballpoint pen
Kunst (f)	art
Kurs (m)	course
Labor (n)	laboratory
Latein	Latin
Lehrer/in (m/f)	teacher
Lehrerzimmer (n)	staffroom
Leistung (f)	achievement
lernen	to learn
Lineal (n)	ruler
Mannschaft (f)	team
Mathe(matik) (f)	maths
Medienwissenschaft	media studies
Mittlere Reife (f)	GCSE equivalent
mündlich	oral
nachsitzen	to have a detention
Naturwissenschaften (pl)	sciences
Note (f)	grade
Oberstufe (f)	sixth form
Pause (f)	break
Physik (f)	physics
Privatschule (f)	private school
Prüfung (f)	exam
Radiergummi (m)	rubber
rechnen	to calculate
Rechner (m)	calculator
Regel (f)	rule
Resultat (n)	result
Schere (f)	scissors
Schreibtisch (m)	desk
schriftlich	written
Schule besuchen	to attend school
Schüler/in (m/f)	pupil
Schülerzeitung (f)	school newspaper
Schulhof (m)	playground
Schultasche (f)	school bag
schwach	weak (subject)
schwer	hard, difficult
Seite (f)	page
Sekretariat (n)	school office
sitzen bleiben	to repeat a year
Sommerferien (pl)	summer holidays
Spanisch	Spanish
Sprache (f)	language
staatlich	state
stark	strong
Stunde (f)	lesson, hour

Stundenplan (m)	timetable
Tafel (f)	board
Taschenrechner (m)	calculator
Theater (n)	drama
Trimester (n)	term
Turnen (n)	gymnastics
Turnhalle (f)	gym
üben	to practise
Übung (f)	exercise
ungerecht	unfair
Unterricht (m)	lesson
unterrichten	to teach
weitermachen	to carry on
Werken (n)	DT
wiederholen	to repeat
Wörterbuch (n)	dictionary
zeichnen	to draw

HIGHER H

abschreiben	to copy
Aufsatz (m)	essay
ausfallen	to be cancelled (lesson)
begabt	gifted
erklären	to explain
Erlaubnis (f)	permission
Internat (n)	boarding school
Klassenbuch (n)	class register
Kopfhörer (m)	headphones
lehren	to teach
Leistungsdruck (m)	pressure to achieve (good grades)
notwendig	necessary
Pflichtfach (n)	core subject
schwänzen	to skive
Strafarbeit (f)	lines (punishment)
Studium (n)	studies
übersetzen	to translate
Übersetzung (f)	translation
vereinbaren	to agree
Wahlfach (n)	optional subject
Wirtschaftslehre (f)	economics

1	= sehr gut	very good
2	= gut	good
3	= befriedigend	satisfactory
4	= ausreichend	adequate
5	= mangelhaft	unsatisfactory, poor
6	= ungenügend	inadequate

Now try this

What GCSEs are you and your friends taking? Check that you can say / write all the subjects in German. If you're thinking of taking A levels, can you name those subjects too?

⑤ Future aspirations, study and work

Further study and work

Add –in for the female word, unless given.

Angestellter (m) / Angestellte (f)	employee
Anruf (m)	call
Arbeiter (m)	worker
Arbeitgeber (m)	employer
Arbeitsbedingungen (pl)	terms of employment
arbeitslos	unemployed
Arbeitspraktikum (n)	work experience
babysitten	to babysit
Bäcker (m)	baker
Bauarbeiter (m)	builder
Bauer (m)	farmer
Beamter (m) / Beamtin (f)	civil servant
Begeisterung (f)	enthusiasm in work
berufstätig	
beschäftigt	busy
Besitzer (m)	owner
Betrieb (m)	business
Betriebspraktikum (n)	work experience
Bezahlung (f)	pay
Bildung (f)	education
Blumenhändler (m)	florist
Briefmarke (f)	stamp
Briefträger (m)	postman
Chef (m)	boss
einstellen	to appoint
Elektriker (m)	electrician
Fabrik (f)	factory
Fähigkeiten (pl)	skills
Fehler (m)	mistake
Ferienjob (m)	holiday job
Feuerwehrfrau (f)	firefighter
Feuerwehrmann (m)	firefighter
Fleischer (m)	butcher
Ganztagsjob (m)	full-time job
Gehalt (n)	salary
Gelegenheit (f)	opportunity
geplant	planned

Hausfrau (f)	housewife
Hausmann (m)	house husband
Hochschulabschluss (m)	degree
Informatik (f)	computer science
jobben	to do casual work
Kassierer (m)	cashier
Kauffrau (f)	businesswoman
Kaufmann (m)	businessman
Klempner (m)	plumber
Kollege / Kollegin	colleague
Künstler (m)	artist
einen Kurs besuchen	to attend a course
lehrreich	educational
Lkw-Fahrer (m)	lorry driver
Lohn (m)	wage(s)
Maler (m)	painter
Maurer (m)	builder
Messe (f)	trade fair
Metzger (m)	butcher
Mitteilung (f), Nachricht (f)	message
Teilzeitjob (m)	part-time job
Polizei (f)	police
Reisebüro (n)	travel agency
Schauspieler (m)	actor
Schichtarbeit (f)	shiftwork
schlecht bezahlt	badly paid
selbstständig	independent
Soldat (m)	soldier
Sorge (f)	worry
Stadtführer (m)	city guide
Streik (m)	strike
Student (m)	student (university)
studieren	to study
Teilzeit (f)	part time
Tellerwäscher (m)	washer-upper
Tierarzt (m) / Tierärztin (f)	vet
Tischler (m)	joiner
Universität (f)	university
verdienen	to earn
Verkäufer (m)	sales assistant
Vertreter (m)	representative
Werkstatt (f)	workshop
Zeitungen austragen	to deliver newspapers

Ziel (n)	aim
zurückrufen	to call back

Arbeitnehmer (m)	employee
Arbeitsamt (n)	job centre
ausrichten	to give a message
Auszubildende (m/f)	trainee
Bewerber (m)	applicant
Dolmetscher (m)	interpreter
Einzelhändler (m)	retailer
Fließband (n)	conveyer belt
freiwillig	voluntary
Gelegenheitsarbeit (f)	casual work
Gesetz (n)	law
Gleichheit (f)	equality
Gleitzeit (f)	flexitime
Hochschulbildung (f)	higher education
Jura	study of law
kündigen	to resign
Landwirt (m)	farmer
Lehrling (m)	apprentice
Medizin (f)	(study of) medicine
Praktikum (n)	internship
Qualifikation (f)	qualification
qualifiziert / ausgebildet	qualified
Rechtsanwalt (m)	lawyer
Schriftsteller (m)	author
sich entschließen	to decide
Unternehmen (n)	firm
vereinbaren	to agree

Volunteering

beschäftigt	busy
freiwillig arbeiten	to work voluntarily
geplant	planned
im Ausland	abroad
Nähen (n)	sewing
organisieren	to organise
Plan (m)	plan
Projekt (n)	project
Schneiderei (f)	tailoring

Now try this

Pick 10 words from this page that you would use when applying for a job. Memorise them and then test yourself later.

⑤ Future aspirations, study and work

Sprache (f)	language
Traum (m)	dream
Wohltätigkeit (f)	charity

freiwillige Arbeit (f)	voluntary work
Freiwilliger (m) / Freiwillige (f)	volunteer
Spendenaktion (f)	charity sale
zu Gunsten	in aid of

der Arzt   die Ärztin

der Bauer   die Bäuerin

der Künstler   die Künstlerin

die Krankenschwester
der Krankenpfleger

der Polizist   die Polizistin

die Zahnärztin   der Zahnarzt

Work

abheften	to file
Akte (f)	file
Aktenmappe (f)	folder
Angestellter (m) / Angestellte (f)	employee
Anrufbeantworter (m)	answerphone
Anzeige (f)	advert
Arbeit (f)	work
Arbeitgeber/in (m/f)	employer
Arbeitsbedingungen (pl)	terms of employment
Arbeitslosigkeit (f)	unemployment
auflegen	to hang up (phone)
Besprechung (f)	meeting
Ehrgeiz (m)	ambition
erfahren	experienced
Formular (n)	form
Gehalt (n)	salary
Gesellschaft (f)	society / company
gut / schlecht bezahlt	well / badly paid
Job (m) / Stelle (f)	job
Kaffeepause (f)	coffee break
Kollege (m) / Kollegin (f)	colleague
Konferenz (f)	conference
Manager/in (m/f)	manager

Marketing (n)	marketing
Mittagspause (f)	lunch break
Nachricht (f)	news
Reisebüro (n)	travel agency
sich um einen Job bewerben	to apply for a job
Stellengesuche (pl)	situations wanted
pro Stunde	per hour
Teepause (f)	tea break
Teilzeit (f)	part time
Telefonanruf (m)	telephone call
Vorstellungsgespräch (n)	interview
wählen	to dial (a number)

Jobs

Apotheker/in (m/f)	pharmacist
Architekt/in (m/f)	architect
Bäcker/in (m/f)	baker
Bauarbeiter/in (m/f)	builder
Beamter (m) / Beamtin (f)	civil servant
Dichter/in (m/f)	poet
Elektriker/in (m/f)	electrician
Fahrer/in (m/f)	driver
Feuerwehrfrau (f)	firefighter
Feuerwehrmann (m)	firefighter
Flugbegleiter/in (m/f)	cabin crew

Informatiker/in (m/f)	computer scientist
Ingenieur/in (m/f)	engineer
Journalist/in (m/f)	journalist
Kassierer/in (m/f)	cashier
Klempner/in (m/f)	plumber
Koch (m) / Köchin (f)	chef
Mechaniker/in (m/f)	mechanic
Metzger/in (m/f)	butcher
Modeschöpfer/in (m/f)	fashion designer
Musiker/in (m/f)	musician
Programmierer/in (m/f)	programmer
Schauspieler/in (m/f)	actor
Techniker/in (m/f)	technician
Vertreter/in (m/f)	sales rep

Aufstiegsmöglichkeiten (pl)	promotion prospects
Beruf (m)	job, profession
Bewerbungsbrief (m)	letter of application
Bewerbungsformular (n)	application form
Eindruck (m)	impression
Stellenangebot (n)	job advert
Termin (m)	appointment
Unterschrift (f)	signature
Ziel (n)	goal

Now try this

To help you learn the jobs vocabulary, make a list of five jobs that you would like to do and five jobs that you would not like to do and then memorise them.

⑥ International and global dimension

Bringing the world together

Aktion (f)	campaign
Armut (f)	poverty
fairer Handel (m)	fair trade
für / gegen	for / against
(Füßball)weltmeisterschaft (f)	world cup (football)
global / weltweit	global
Hunger (m)	hunger
Katastrophe (f) / Unglück (n)	catastrophe
Krieg (m)	war
Land (n)	country
leben	to live
Mangel (m) (an)	lack (of)
Menschen (pl) / Leute (pl)	people
Musikfest (n)	music festival
Nachteil (m)	disadvantage
die Olympischen Spiele (pl)	Olympic Games
Schutz (m)	protection
sterben	to die
Vorteil (m)	advantage
Wohltätigkeitsverein (m)	charity

bedürftig	needy
fehlen	to lack
Menschenrechte (pl)	human rights
profitieren	to profit
retten	to rescue
Sicherheit (f)	security
Spionage (f)	spying
überleben	to survive
unglucklich	unfortunate
unmittelbar	instant

Environmental issues

recyceln	die Welt
to recycle	the world

Dürre (f)	drought
Energie (f)	energy
Erde (f)	earth
Hungersnot (f)	famine
Müll (m)	rubbish
Naturschätze (pl)	natural resources
Orkan (m)	hurricane
Planet (m)	planet
Regenwald (m)	rainforest
Schutz (m)	protection
schützen	to protect
Strom (m)	electricity
Trinkwasser (n)	drinking water
Überschwemmung (f)	flooding
Umwelt (f)	environment
Verschmutzung (f)	pollution

Art (f)	species
drohen	to threaten
Erdbeben (n)	earthquake
frisches Wasser (n) / Süßwasser (n)	fresh water
globale Erwärmung (f)	global warming
Klima (n)	climate
kompostieren	to compost
Solarenergie (f)	solar energy
trennen	to separate (rubbish)
verschmutzen, vergiften	to pollute / poison
Vulkan (m)	volcano

Kohle (f)	Gas (n)	Öl (n)
coal	gas	oil

Tiere (pl)	Salzwasser (n)	Pflanzen (npl)
animals	salt water	plants

Now try this

Choose 10 words and make learning cards for them – English or a photo on one side and German on the other.

Answers

The answers to the Speaking and Writing activities below are sample answers – there are many ways you could answer these questions.

Identity and culture

1. Physical descriptions
(a) zwanzig
(b) lang
(c) ein Piercing
(d) Kleidung
(e) sprechen

2. Character descriptions
(a) faul
(b) freundlich
(c) laut
(d) laut
(e) lustig

4. Friends
(a) Meine Freundin Carol ist klug / intelligent und sehr lustig.
(b) Ich sehe meine Freunde / Freundinnen oft nach der Schule.
(c) Letzte Woche gab mein Freund eine Party.
(d) Meine beste Freundin hat in Spanien gewohnt, als sie acht Jahre alt war.

5. Role models
(a) depends on the tastes/interests of the person
(b) improve own skills/reach sporting goals
(c) any two: teachers, naturalists/nature protectors, scientists, authors

6. Relationships
(a) Lehrer
(b) 45
(c) viermal
(d) Freunde
(e) mag

7. When I was younger

9. Customs

10. Home
My parents are old-fashioned and we always have to have lunch together and chat because mobile phones and other electronic devices are banned at the table. It is my dream to live alone in the city centre, so that I can have my own house rules. As a child I lived in the countryside, but that was terribly dull because there was nothing to do in the evenings. I would never like to live in such a place again!

11. Everyday life
(b) their everyday life has become so technical
(c) any two: managers had a secretary / office to plan for them / assistants for technical matters / were not going through puberty
(d) everything themselves

12. Meals at home
(a) Frühstück
(b) Kaffee und Kuchen
(c) Abendessen
(d) Mittagessen
(e) Kaffee und Kuchen

14. Shopping for clothes

15. Social media
A, C and F

17. Online activities
(b) her parents find it particularly important
(c) talks for hours on mobile phone
(d) any two: turns on tablet / uploads funny photos / waits for comments
(e) she only wants to get positive comments

19. Hobbies
(a) D
(b) A
(c) C

20. Interests
Yesterday I went with my family to the cinema. You would find the film boring, because the special effects were old-fashioned.

22. Sport

23. Reading
(b) made them look tiny
(c) nothing
(d) any two: she saw so little / it was tiring / she only read one letter each day

25. Television
(a) lustig
(b) blöd
(c) interessant
(d) entspannend
(e) lustig

26. Celebrations
(a) cake
(b) often
(c) money
(d) drinks
(e) works

27. Festivals
Als mein Freund eine Faschingsparty gab, hat diese mir gar nicht gefallen und ich bin früh nach Hause gegangen. Dieses Jahr werde ich zu Silvester in die Stadtmitte fahren, weil eine Band auf dem Marktplatz spielen wird und wir dort tanzen können. Ich möchte am liebsten mit einer großen Menge im Freien feiern.

Local area, holiday and travel

29. Hotels

(a) Bett
(b) viel
(c) online
(d) regelmäßig
(e) plant

30. Campsites

C, E and G

31. Accommodation

Listen to the recording

32. Holiday destinations

As a family we go every year to Tenerife, where we always spend our first day in the biggest water park in Europe. I would also recommend a day trip to the capital, in order to visit the wonderful markets and buy lots of cheap souvenirs. We have been going there for four years and before we came here, we had always spent our summer holiday by / at the windy North Sea.

33. Holiday experiences

(a) fantastisch
(b) enttäuschend
(c) interessant

34. Holiday activities

(b) any one: archery / climbing / waterskiing
(c) go for walks
(d) a day trip
(e) will come back

35. Holiday plans

Als ich letztes Mal dort war, habe ich einige echt nette Leute kennengelernt. Wir werden uns wieder im Mai treffen und alle einen Tagesausflug zum See machen. Ich möchte lieber Urlaub mit Freunden als mit meiner / der Familie machen, weil mir das besser gefällt.

36. Holiday problems

Listen to the recording

37. Asking for help

Listen to the recording

39. Travel

(b) much better than in England
(c) if we invested more in trains

40. Directions

(a) D
(b) C
(c) A

41. Eating in a café

Last time my mother ordered a fried egg. Next time she will not order that again.

42. Eating in a restaurant

(a) B
(b) D
(c) A

43. Shopping for food

(a) Petra
(b) Alex
(c) Kai
(d) Edi
(e) Petra

44. Opinions about food

(b) waiter was very rude / not at all polite
(c) would recommend restaurant for wonderful views and 10% reduction for students

45. Buying gifts

(b) wonderful shop windows
(c) they sell gold watches / silk linen
(d) the very tall houses

46. Weather

(a) D
(b) A

47. Places to see

(b) one of the most popular tourist destinations
(c) it is a small town
(d) one of the oldest buildings in the town (**not**: old building / historic)
(e) in the town centre

48. At the tourist office

Listen to the recording

49. Describing a town

(a) Das Kaufhaus ist sehr alt und teuer.
(b) Ich gehe lieber am Markt einkaufen.
(c) Gestern bin ich ins Kino gegangen.
(d) Mein Bruder ist zu Hause geblieben, weil er müde war / denn er war müde.

50. Describing a region

D, E and C

51. Tourism

Listen to the recording

School

53. School subjects

(b) A
(c) B

54. Opinions about school

Listen to the recording

55. School day

C, E and G

57. School facilities

Listen to the recording

58. School rules

Last term a pupil / student smoked in the playground, because he thought that was cool. But the head teacher was very angry and sent the boy straight home. I would never smoke or drink alcohol at school, because I wouldn't want to get a detention.

59. Pressures at school

Obwohl Schüler / Schülerinnen heutzutage oft Klassenarbeiten schreiben müssen, können wir uns noch echt auf die Klassenfahrten freuen. Wenn ich fleißig lerne, um gute Noten zu bekommen, werde ich auch vielleicht eine Belohnung von meinen Eltern bekommen – und das wird sich lohnen!

60. Primary school

C

61. Success at school

(b)   D

63. School exchange

Listen to the recording

64. School events

(a)   C, E   (b)   B, D

Future aspirations, study and work

65. Future study

Listen to the recording

66. Jobs

(b)   any one: Saturday job / cashier / in a shoe shop
(c)   any one: works long hours / exhausted after work / has no time for hobbies (**not:** she's a doctor)
(d)   works in a hut in the garden / collects original ties (**not:** he is funny / collects originals)

67. Professions

Last weekend she worked hard. Next year she will apply for a new job.

68. Job wishes

(a)   variety   (b)   salary, travel

69. Opinions about jobs

2	Negative	7	Positive and negative
3	Positive and negative	8	Positive and negative
4	Positive and negative	9	Negative
5	Negative	10	Positive
6	Positive		

70. Job adverts

(b)   Mein Freund / Meine Freundin verdient zwei Euro pro Stunde.
(c)   Er arbeitet in einem Büro in der Stadtmitte.
(d)   Letztes Jahr habe ich als Kellner/in gearbeitet.
(e)   Ich brauche einen Job, weil ich kein Geld habe.

71. Applying for a job

(a)   A   (b)   D

72. Job interview

Listen to the recording

73. Languages beyond the classroom

(b)   seine Sprachkenntnisse sind nicht gut genug / mangelnde Sprachkenntnisse / man muss in der Sprache fließend sein (not: er hat zwei Sprachen / Portugiesisch / Finnisch gelernt)
(c)   any one: mit deutlichen Pausen sprechen / zu langsam verstehen oder reagieren / undeutlich sprechen (not: sofort reagieren / Informationen schnell verarbeiten / das Gesagte klar und flüssig wiedergeben)

74. Volunteering

(a)   C and E   (b)   A and E

75. Training

Listen to the recording

International and global dimension

78. Global sports events

Obwohl Brasilien ein armes Land ist, hatte man ein wunderbares Leichtathletikstadion gebaut und viele Menschen hatten Eintrittskarten gekauft. Das Ziel eines Sportlers oder einer Sportlerin ist es bestimmt, eine Medaille bei einer Meisterschaft zu gewinnen.

79. Global music events

Listen to the recording

80. Being green

(b) A   **(c)** D   **(d)** B

81. Protecting the environment

(b) Klimawechsel zu vermeiden (**not**: seinen Effekt zu begrenzen / Strategien zu entwickeln)

(c) uns daran anpassen / uns an den Klima anpassen (not: seinen Effekt zu begrenzen / Strategien entwickeln)

(d) Menschen / Leute haben eine große Rolle dabei gespielt (not: negative Folgen)

(e) extremes Wetter (not: any of the individual weather types)

(f) die Berge / die Alpen

83. Campaigns

A and E

Grammar

85. Gender and plurals

(a) die Anmeldung / die Anmeldungen
(b) der Fahrer / die Fahrer
(c) das Rührei / die Rühreier
(d) die Haltestelle / die Haltestellen
(e) der Fernseher / die Fernseher
(f) das Brötchen / die Brötchen

86. Cases and prepositions

(a) gegen die Mauer
(b) außer einem Kind
(c) trotz des Schnees
(d) nach einer Stunde
(e) zu den Geschäften
(f) ohne ein Wort
(g) während des Sommers
(h) beim Arzt

87. Dative and accusative prepositions

(a) der
(b) den
(c) dem
(d) die
(e) der
(f) den
(g) den
(h) die

88. Dieser / jeder, kein / mein

(a) I don't want to go shopping.
(b) She spent all her pocket money on clothes.
(c) Such people quickly become impolite.
(d) I find my life boring.
(e) This time we are going by train.
(f) His parents are unemployed.
(g) I find such rules stupid.
(h) Which book are you reading?

89. Adjective endings

(a) ausgezeichnete
(b) warmes
(c) preisgünstiges
(d) zentrale
(e) beliebtes
(f) meistverkauften
(g) verkaufsoffenen
(h) persönlichen

90. Comparisons

(a) einfacher
(b) jünger
(c) besser
(d) nützlicher
(e) winzigste
(f) langweiligste
(g) beliebteste
(h) schlechtesten

91. Personal pronouns

(a) sie
(b) mir
(c) dir
(d) uns
(e) mir, ihm
(f) mir

92. Word order

Possible answers:

(a) Ich fahre gern ins Ausland.
(b) Man findet Informationen beim Verkehrsamt.
(c) Normalerweise esse ich gesund.
(d) Manchmal sehen wir im Jugendklub Filme.
(e) Im Juli möchte ich im Sportzentrum arbeiten.
(f) Letztes Jahr habe ich in einem Büro gearbeitet.
(g) Morgen werde ich mit meiner Mutter ins Kino gehen.

93. Conjunctions

(a) Ich habe bei meiner Großmutter gewohnt, während meine Mutter im Krankenhaus war.

(b) Ich bin ins Café gegangen, nachdem ich ein T-Shirt gekauft habe.

(c) Ich war in Spanien im Urlaub, als ich einen neuen Freund kennengelernt habe.

(d) Er ist sehr beliebt, obwohl er nicht sehr freundlich ist.

(e) Ich werde für eine neue Gitarre sparen, wenn ich einen Nebenjob finde.

(f) Ich bin froh, dass ich gute Noten in der Schule bekommen habe.

(g) Ich muss meine Eltern fragen, ob ich ins Konzert gehen darf.

(h) Er hat mir gesagt, dass er mit mir ins Kino gehen will.

94. More on word order

1 **(a)** Ich fahre nach Italien, um meine Verwandten zu besuchen.
  (b) Ich gehe zum Sportzentrum, um 5 Kilo abzunehmen.
2 **(a)** Ich versuche, anderen zu helfen.
  (b) Ich habe vor, auf die Uni zu gehen.
3 **(a)** Das ist das Geschäft, das tolle Kleidung verkauft.
  (b) Hier ist eine Kellnerin, die sehr unhöflich ist.

95. The present tense

(a) höre
(b) schläft
(c) geht
(d) Isst
(e) fahren
(f) machen
(g) Gibt
(h) bleibt

96. Separable and reflexive verbs

1 **(a)** Ich sehe fern. Ich habe ferngesehen.
  (b) Ich steige um sechs Uhr um. Ich bin um sechs Uhr umgestiegen.
  (c) Ich lade Musik herunter. Ich werde Musik herunterladen.
  (d) Ich bin eingestiegen. Ich muss einsteigen.
2 **(a)** mich
  (b) uns
  (c) euch
  (d) sich

97. Commands

To pay attention to their darlings and not to use the green spaces and paths as a dog toilet.

98. Present tense modals

(a) Ich muss um einundzwanzig Uhr ins Bett gehen.
(b) In der Schule darf man nicht rauchen.
(c) Du sollst Energie sparen.
(d) Kannst du mir zu Hause helfen?
(e) Ich will in den Ferien Ski fahren.
(f) Ich möchte nicht fernsehen.
(g) Ich kann das Problem nicht lösen.

99. Imperfect modals

1 (a) Ich musste Hausaufgaben machen.
  (b) Sie konnten mir nicht helfen.
  (c) Er wollte eine neue Hose kaufen.
  (d) Wir sollten die Fotos hochladen.
  (e) In der Schule durfte man nie Kaugummi kauen.
  (f) Alle Schüler mussten bis sechzehn Uhr bleiben.
2 (a) Es könnte schwierig werden.
  (b) Ich möchte die gelbe Jacke umtauschen.

100. The perfect tense 1

(a) Ich habe eine Jacke gekauft.
(b) Wir sind nach Portugal geflogen.
(c) Ich habe meinen Freund gesehen.
(d) Lena und Hannah sind in die Stadt gegangen.
(e) Ich habe meine Tante besucht.
(f) Ich bin im Hotel geblieben.
(g) Was hast du zu Mittag gegessen?
(h) Am Samstag hat er Musik gehört.

101. The perfect tense 2

(a) Ich habe zu viele Kekse gegessen.
(b) Haben Sie gut geschlafen?
(c) Wir haben uns am Bahnhof getroffen.
(d) Ich war krank, weil ich den ganzen Tag gestanden habe.
(e) Ich weiß, dass du umgestiegen bist.
(f) Warum hast du die E-Mail geschrieben?
(g) Ich habe ihr empfohlen, dass sie nicht mitkommen sollte.
(h) Ich war traurig, als er gestorben ist.

102. The imperfect tense

(a) Sie hatte Angst.
(b) Es war hoffnungslos.
(c) Es gab Toiletten im Erdgeschoss.
(d) Hörtest du das?
(e) Plötzlich kam uns der Mann entgegen.
(f) Das war eine Überraschung, nicht?
(g) Es war niemand zu Hause.
(h) Sie spielten gern Tischtennis.

103. The future tense

(a) Ich werde das Spiel gewinnen.
(b) Wir werden in den Freizeitpark gehen.
(c) Sie werden eine große Wohnung mieten.
(d) Ihr werdet große Schwierigkeiten haben.
(e) Er wird die Prüfung bestehen.
(f) Nächste Woche werden wir umziehen.
(g) Werdet ihr euch später treffen?
(h) Ich werde mich um sechs Uhr anziehen.

104. The conditional

(a) Ich würde gern ins Theater gehen.
(b) Er würde nie zu spät ankommen.
(c) Wir würden nie Bier trinken.
(d) Würden Sie mir bitte helfen?
(e) Zum Geburtstag würde sie am liebsten Geld bekommen.
(f) Nächstes Jahr würden sie vielleicht heiraten.
(g) Wenn Latein Pflicht wäre, würde ich auf eine andere Schule gehen.
(h) Wenn ich das machen würde, gäbe es Krach mit meinen Eltern.

105. The pluperfect tense

(a) Ich hatte zu Mittag gegessen.
(b) Sie hatten als Stadtführer gearbeitet.
(c) Warst du schwimmen gegangen?
(d) Wir waren in Kontakt geblieben.
(e) Sie waren mit dem Rad in die Stadt gefahren.
(f) Ich hatte sie vor einigen Monaten besucht, aber damals war sie schon krank.
(g) Bevor ich ins Haus gegangen war, hatte ich ein Gesicht am Fenster gesehen.
(h) Obwohl ich kaum mit ihm gesprochen hatte, schien er sehr freundlich zu sein.

106. Questions

1 (a) Lesen Sie gern Science-Fiction-Bücher?
  (b) Finden Sie Ihre Arbeit anstrengend?
  (c) Möchten Sie nur Teilzeit arbeiten?
  (d) Werden Sie nächsten Sommer nach Australien auswandern?
2 (a) Wer könnte mir helfen?
  (b) Wann macht das Restaurant auf?
  (c) Warum gibt es eine Tasche hier?
  (d) Wie komme ich zum Dom?
  (e) Was kann man abends machen?

107. Time markers

(a) Seit drei Jahren spiele ich Klavier.
(b) Letzte Woche hat er die Hausaufgaben nicht gemacht.
(c) Nächsten Sommer werden wir in den Bergen wandern gehen.
(d) Am Anfang wollten wir das Betriebspraktikum nicht machen.
(e) In Zukunft wird man alle Lebensmittel elektronisch kaufen.
(f) Ich hoffe, eines Tages Disneyland zu besuchen.
(g) Vorgestern hatte ich Halsschmerzen.
(h) Früher haben sie / Sie oft Tennis gespielt.

108. Numbers

(a) 14.–23. Mai
(b) 07:45
(c) €3,80
(d) 27. Januar 1756
(e) €185 Millionen
(f) 15% Ermäßigung
(g) 16:35
(h) 35 Grad

114. Vocabulary

(a) Bavaria
(b) English Channel
(c) Lake Constance
(d) Black Forest
(e) Alps
(f) Danube
(g) Geneva
(h) Cologne
(i) Munich
(j) Vienna

Published by Pearson Education Limited, 80 Strand, London, WC2R 0RL.

www.pearsonschoolsandfecolleges.co.uk

Text and illustrations © Pearson Education Limited 2016
Produced, typeset and illustrations by Cambridge Publishing Management Ltd
Cover illustration by Miriam Sturdee

The rights of Harriette Lanzer to be identified as author of this work have been asserted by her in accordance with the Copyright, Designs and Patents Act 1988.

First published 2016

19 18 17

10 9 8 7 6 5 4 3 2

British Library Cataloguing in Publication Data
A catalogue record for this book is available from the British Library

ISBN 978 1 2921 3209 9

Printed in Slovakia by Neografia.

Acknowledgements
The publisher would like to thank the following for their kind permission to reproduce their photographs:

(Key: b-bottom; c-centre; l-left; r-right; t-top)

123RF.com: Dmitriy Shironosov 13, 29, Graham Oliver 30; **Alamy Images:** Agencja Fotograficzna Caro 49, Cultura Creative (RF) 107; **Fotolia.com:** airmaria 84, Artem Merzlenko 66tr, davit85 62, Halfpoint 79, John Smith 26, kristina rütten 38, Phase4Photography 70, Syda Productions 100, TEMISTOCLE LUCARELLI 66cr, V&P Photo Studio 69, WavebreakMediaMicro 98; **Getty Images:** Siri Stafford 56; **Imagestate Media:** John Foxx Collection 51; **Pearson Education Ltd:** Lord and Leverett 75tr, Sophie Bluy 59, 104cl, 104cr; **PhotoDisc:** 55; **Shutterstock.com:** Alexander Raths 67, Andre Blais 95, dotshock 22, fonzales 16, Goodluz 57, IM_photo 28, infografick 45, Jefferson Bernardes 78, Joshua Haviv 35, Maksym Gorpenyuk 31, Martin Valigursky 32, Masson 2, Mikadun 47, Monkey Business Images 7, RoxyFer 21, runzelkorn 75bl, Sergey Kohl 83, SpeedKingz 61, Vicki L. Miller 74, View Apart 48; **www.imagesource.com:** 34

All other images © Pearson Education

We are grateful to the following for permission to reproduce copyright material:

Worked Example on page 11 adapted from Jugendliche haben einen Alltag wie früher Manager, *Die Welt*, 29/06/2014 (Krauel T.), http://www.welt.de/debatte/kommentare/article129580927/Jugendliche-haben-einen-Alltag-wie-frueher-Manager.html; Worked Example on page 15 adapted from http://www.jugendundmedien.ch/chancen-und-gefahren/soziale-netzwerke.html; Worked Example on page 23 from *Paula die Leseratte*, Verlag Razamba (Ebbertz, M. 2010) p.5; Worked Example on page 45 from *Emil und die Detektive*, Cecilie Dressler Verlag (Kastner, E. 1991) p.67; Worked Example on page 55 adapted from *Stundenplan*, Beltz & Gelberg (Nöstlinger,C. 2014) 9; Worked Example on page 73 adapted from *Übersetzen und Dolmetschen: Mit Sprachen arbeiten ISBN 978-92-79-12047-3*, Amt für Veröff entlichungen der Europäischen Union (2009) p.3, 5, adapted from the original document published on http://bookshop.europa.eu/de/uebersetzen-und-dolmetschen-pbHC3212079/ © European Union, 2009. Responsibility for the adaptation lies entirely with Pearson Education Ltd., © European Union, 1995-2015; Worked Example on page 81 adapted from *50 einfache Dinge, die Sie tun können, um die Welt zu retten*, Heyne Verlag (Schlumberger, A/ 2006) p.13